kids'
kitchen

Amanda Grant

kids'
kitchen

MITCHELL BEAZLEY

Kids' Kitchen
Good food made easy

First published in Great Britain in 2005 by Mitchell Beazley, an imprint of Octopus Publishing Group Limited, 2–4 Heron Quays, London E14 4JP.
© Octopus Publishing Group Limited 2005
Text © Amanda Grant 2005

A CIP catalogue record for this book is available from the British Library.

ISBN 184 000 889 X

Commissioning Editors: Vivien Antwi and Rebecca Spry
Executive Art Editor: Yasia Williams
Design: Tim Pattinson
Editors: Vanessa Kendell and Rebecca Spry
Home Economy Assistant: Sibilla Whitehead
Photography: Francesca Yorke
Production: Seyhan Esen
Index: John Noble

Colour reproduction by Bright Arts

Printed and bound by Toppan Printing Company in China

For Ella, Jasmin and Finn X

Thanks Becca, this is the book I have always wanted to write, you are truly wonderful to work with. Thanks David for believing in everything I do. Pop, you and mummy gave me a brilliant childhood – for that I will always be grateful. Thanks for always being there.

Vicki, you star for introducing me to Becca, I do miss seeing you. To all my friends, especially Billy, for all your tireless help; Amanda, Annie, Kate, Liz and Lou for testing recipes, recipe ideas and just listening. Milly, thanks for your recipe testing, and I hope you continue to enjoy cooking the recipes with your friends.

Fran, what can I say, a photo shoot I will never forget! A huge thank you to you for the totally gorgeous pictures. Thanks to Tim and Yasia – it really does look fantastic.

A big thank you to all the local 'amateur' models – Alice, Archie, Bea, Charlie, Edward, Ella, Emily, Jack, Jacob, Jake, Jasmin, Kirsty, Lucia, Rosa, Tamas, Teddy, Tilly, William, Zoe, and to all the models from Alphabet Kidz – Iman, Louis, Mae, Morgan and Usman – you really have helped make this book come to life, well done to all of you!

Diona, Vivien and Vanessa, phew – thanks for all your stirling efforts.

Finally, a quick thanks to my local shops for helping me cook good food, especially to Bill and his team at Bill's Food Store; all the guys (and Petrina) at Frank Richards Butcher's; and Vera and Arran at the Lewes Fruit Store.

6 introduction and good kitchen practice

introduction

for mum and dad

I am totally passionate about getting children into the kitchen. They need to be able to get messy with food, to touch, smell and learn about food, and one of the best ways to do this is to let them cook. This does not have to mean that your child spends hours baking, leaving behind him a wake of destruction. It can be that he just starts by helping you with simple tasks, such as crushing garlic or whisking egg whites. My youngest is eighteen months and he loves to hold the electric whisk with me when I am whisking egg whites, although I am sure it is the noise from the whisk that excites him more than anything else!

However, learning about food does not just involve cooking, it also means having an understanding of where food comes from.

This book is for children, it is their recipe book to keep, use and refer to over and over. Once they have mastered some of the basic techniques explained here, they will be able to cook good food pretty much anywhere. If children are given the chance to have a go at making food for themselves and their family or friends, they are also more likely to enjoy eating a wide variety of foods.

for you

I have been involved with good food for as long as I can remember. My mother was an excellent cook and she enthused about really good quality food and the joy of cooking for family and friends. I loved cooking from a very young age and by the grand old age of six I was selling cakes to my mother's friends for extra pocket money.

I remember being allowed to collect fresh eggs from the hens on our local farm and being so excited when we cooked them for breakfast. Have you ever been to a farm? If not, ask your mum or dad if you could go to see the animals and chickens, or visit a working dairy to see the cows being milked. Don't be afraid to ask questions, such as how many eggs hens lay or what they eat or what happens to the milk once it leaves the dairy.

Farmers' markets are also a great way to learn about food and what we eat. The person selling the food is often the person who produces it, so you will find that he knows a lot about his produce.

A big part of my childhood was spent shopping for food from our local butcher, baker, greengrocer and fishmonger, from whom I learned a great deal about where food comes from. Shopping, whether it is in a supermarket or local food shop, is a big part of our every day life, so try to enjoy it. Even your younger brothers or sisters can have fun going to get things off the shelves and putting them into the trolley or counting out fruit and vegetables into bags. Ask your mum or dad if you can be given the responsibility of choosing food, such as a cut of meat or some fresh fish.

Once you have helped to shop for your food you can think about cooking. Just as when you started to read you learned the sound of letters before putting them together to make words, when you start to cook it is a good idea to learn some of the basic techniques first, which you can then use to make a whole variety of dishes. For example, once you know how to whisk you can make meringues, fruit fools and chocolate mousse. Learning how to rub butter into flour means you can make pastry as well as biscuits and crumble toppings.

There are so many skills to learn in this book, but most importantly, have fun in the kitchen and enjoy eating – and sharing – the good food that you have made.

good kitchen practice

GETTING STUCK IN

Before you get stuck in, have a quick read through the following and check with your mum or dad that it is OK for you to do some cooking. Read the recipes before you start and try to get all your ingredients weighed out and your equipment ready. You will find it easier when you start cooking, and you can always pretend to be a professional chef – with everything ready to hand! When I was eight years old, I used to make my brothers sit and watch me cook so that I could pretend to be on television!

WEIGHING AND MEASURING

Each recipe gives both metric and imperial measures. However, when you are weighing out your ingredients you should always stick to just one for the whole recipe. Ideally make sure that it is metric – all foods are sold in metric measures and metric weights are given on packets nowadays.

SCALES

I have not mentioned scales on the equipment list for each recipe as I am presuming that you will have a set and that you will use them as and when necessary. I particularly like the electronic ones which are easy to read, even for toddlers who need some help with their number skills!

MEASURING JUG

Your scales may have a liquid measure, which enables you to measure liquids straight into saucepans or bowls. Alternatively you may need to use a measuring jug, which can be plastic, enamel or glass.

SPOONS

If possible, try to use measuring teaspoons and tablespoons, which are available from large supermarkets or good cook shops. A heaped spoon can contain double the amount of a level spoon, so keep an eye on this – it's especially important if you are baking.

EQUIPMENT

Hopefully you will have most things needed for the recipes in your kitchen already, and I am sure that in most cases you can improvise if you do not have the exact thing. A hand-held blender is a particularly useful piece of equipment. They do not cost a lot of money and you can use them for many different things, such as smoothies, soups and fruit purées to mix with yoghurt. A vegetable peeler with an easy-to-grip handle is also very useful.

OVEN

You may have noticed that there are many different types of oven. Some have gas hobs (the top of the oven where you rest the saucepan, frying pan, etc) and others are electric. Some ovens are gas and similarly, others are electric. Most electric ovens have a little red light that goes out when the oven is at the right temperature. The more cooking you do, the more you will get to know how your oven works. You may need to vary the cooking time slightly to suit your oven – some ovens cook food more quickly than others and your food may be cooked in 15 minutes even if the recipe says 20.

You will need to check your food before the recommended cooking time is up just in case it is cooking quickly. Remember to turn your oven on 10–15 minutes before you need it because it can take a little while to warm up, and remember to turn it off when you have finished.

Easy guide to oven temperatures
110°C/225°F/gas mark ¼
120°C/250°F/gas mark ½
140°C/275°F/gas mark 1
150°C/300°F/gas mark 2
170°C/325°F/gas mark 3
180°C/350°F/gas mark 4
190°C/375°F/gas mark 5
200°C/400°F/gas mark 6
220°C/425°F/gas mark 7
230°C/450°F/gas mark 8
240°C/475°F/gas mark 9

A WORD ON SAFETY
To stay safe in the kitchen, please spend 5 minutes reading through this section.

- Knives and the blades of blenders and food processors are sharp. Always check with your mum or dad before using them and handle them very carefully.
- Ovens, grills and hobs can get very hot – always wear oven gloves when you are putting things into the oven or grill or taking them out.
- Be careful when you are stirring hot things in pans. Keep your hands, arms and face a safe distance away from boiling water or steam.
- Keep paper towels or kitchen towels away from the hob.
- If you drop anything on the floor pick it up and wipe it up to prevent anyone from slipping on it.
- Turn pan handles to the side of the cooker so that the pans don't get knocked off the hob.
- Always ask your mum or dad to help you carry heavy pans or tip food into a colander or serving dish.

A WORD ON HYGIENE
- Pop an apron on before you begin – not only does this stop you from getting your clothes all covered in food, but it stops any dirt, paint, etc from falling off your clothes and into your food.
- Wash your hands before you start cooking.
- Tie back your hair if it is long.
- Try to use different chopping boards for different foods – for example, keep one for meats, one for fruit and vegetables, etc. If this is not possible, please wash them thoroughly in-between jobs.
- Make sure that the ingredients you use are within their 'use-by' date.
- Only reheat cooked foods once and make sure they are piping hot all the way through to the middle.

A FEW FINAL THINGS
Look after your kitchen – put hot dishes, straight from the oven, on to mats so that you do not damage your work-surface. Clear up when you have finished – it can be fun washing everything down with a cloth and soapy water!

1 FROM THE SEA

pan-frying fish

Pan-frying, or frying in the minimum of fat, is suitable for a variety of fish, particularly white fish, such as plaice, sole, cod, bass and haddock and some oily fish, such as salmon, trout and mackerel. Frying in butter gives fish a lovely flavour, but butter burns easily. Mixing butter with oil makes it possible to heat it to a higher temperature. You can pan-fry fillets of fish or smaller whole fish.

plaice with herb butter

SERVES 4

YOU WILL NEED:

INGREDIENTS
- 50g (1¾oz) butter, softened
- 2 tbsp parsley, finely chopped
- a large pinch of salt and freshly ground black pepper
- 4 thin fillets white fish, such as plaice
- 2 tbsp plain flour
- 2 tbsp olive oil
- lemon wedges, to serve

EQUIPMENT
- bowl
- small wooden spoon
- greaseproof paper
- knife
- 2 large plates
- large frying pan
- fish slice

1 Put 30g (1oz) of the butter in a bowl and, using a small wooden spoon, beat until soft. Mix in the parsley and a pinch of salt and pepper.

2 Scoop the butter on to a piece of greaseproof paper. Fold the paper tightly over the butter and roll it into a sausage shape. Put the butter in the refrigerator.

3 Unless your fish is boneless, run your finger over it to check for bones. If you find any, cut them out with a knife.

4 Put the flour on to a plate and mix in a pinch of salt and pepper. Dip each fillet in the flour and shake off the excess. Put the fillets on a clean plate.

5 Heat the oil and remaining butter in a frying pan until it starts to bubble. Pan-fry the fish for 3–4 minutes, Ⓐ then turn with a fish slice (don't move the fish before this time as it may have stuck to the pan) and fry for a further 3–4 minutes, depending on the thickness of your fish, until cooked. When fish is cooked it changes from see-through to white, the flesh is firmer, it flakes easily and the edges should be turning pale golden brown.

6 Using a fish slice, lift each piece of fish on to a warm plate. Cut the butter log into eight slices and put two slices on top of each piece of fish. Serve with lemon wedges.

shallow-frying fish

Shallow-frying uses more fat than pan-frying, and oil is used instead of a combination of oil and butter. The frying pan is filled with about 1cm (½ inch) of oil. White fish, such as plaice, haddock and cod, or little oily fish, such as sardines and herrings, are often shallow-fried. The fish tends to be cut into bite-sized pieces or small fillets before frying, but you can use tiny whole fish. The fish is coated in seasoned flour, then beaten egg, and then dipped in breadcrumbs, oatmeal or polenta. This protects the flesh from the heat and gives it a lovely crisp coating. The best oil to use is something flavourless, such as sunflower oil.

to shallow-fry fish:

1 Pour the oil into a frying pan – it should be about 1cm (½ inch) deep.

2 Put the pan over a medium heat. The oil needs to be quite hot so that the outside of the fish gets crisp and golden but the inside is less well cooked. To test the oil, drop a small cube of bread into it Ⓐ – if it sizzles you know the oil is ready.

3 Spread your seasoned flour on a plate, put your beaten egg in a shallow bowl, and put some breadcrumbs (see page 25) on a plate.

4 Rinse the boneless fish under cold water. Put it on to kitchen paper and pat dry. If you are cooking a fish fillet, cut it in half lengthways.

5 Dip the fish first in the seasoned flour and shake off any excess, then in the beaten egg before letting any excess drip back into the bowl, then in the breadcrumbs, using your hands to sprinkle the crumbs over it so it is completely covered.

6 Using a fish slice, add the fish to the pan. Cook for 3–4 minutes, depending on its thickness, then use a fish slice to gently turn it and cook until it is golden all over. You can cook more than one fillet half at a time if there is room in your pan.

7 Lift the fish out using a fish slice and put it on to a plate lined with kitchen paper, which will absorb any excess oil. Cover with foil to keep warm.

8 Cook the remaining fish in batches. Serve with lemon wedges.

shallow-frying fish

Adding a little lemon rind to the breadcrumb coating helps to bring out the flavour of the fish. Try serving these fish fingers with some mayonnaise mixed with a little lemon juice.

lemony fish fingers

MAKES APPROX 16 (APPROX 4 SERVINGS)

YOU WILL NEED:

INGREDIENTS

- 6 tbsp plain flour
- a pinch of salt and freshly ground black pepper
- very finely grated zest of ½ lemon
- 1 large egg
- 1 tbsp cold water
- 120g (4¼oz) dried breadcrumbs (see page 25)
- 450g (1lb) boneless white fish fillets, such as cod or haddock
- 150–250ml (5–9fl oz) sunflower oil
- a small cube of bread

EQUIPMENT

- lemon zester
- 4 large plates
- shallow bowl
- fork
- kitchen paper
- knife
- chopping board
- frying pan
- slotted spoon

1 Put the flour on to a plate and mix in a pinch of salt and pepper and the lemon zest. Crack the egg by tapping it firmly against the side of a shallow bowl, pushing your thumbs into the crack and carefully pulling the shell apart, letting the egg drop into the bowl. Add the water and beat well with a fork. Put the breadcrumbs on a plate.

2 Check the fish for bones and pat dry with kitchen paper.

3 Using a knife and a chopping board, cut the fish into strips as thick as your thumb but a little longer.

4 Dip a piece of fish into the flour, then the egg, then the breadcrumbs (see page 13, point 5). Lay on a clean plate.

5 Do the same with all the other pieces of fish – once you get going you can do a few at a time so it doesn't take too long. Wash and dry your hands.

6 (A) Shallow-fry the fish until cooked (see page 13, points 6–8). Eat straight away.

roasting fish

Roasting – cooking in the oven with a little fat – is a quick and easy way to cook fish. The oven is turned on to a high setting so that the fish cooks quickly, keeping the flesh moist. But the high heat can dry out the flesh, so it is best to use thicker fish, such as salmon, cod, bass, and haddock, and be careful not to overcook it. To keep the fish moist, a little fat is added – a drizzle of olive oil or a few dots of butter. Unless you want the fish to have a crisp crust, as in the recipe below, cover your roasting dish with a piece of foil before putting it in the oven.

roast salmon with an orange crust

SERVES 4

YOU WILL NEED:

INGREDIENTS
- approx 15ml (½fl oz) olive oil
- 4 boneless salmon fillets, approx 2.5cm (1 inch) thick
- a large pinch of salt and freshly ground black pepper
- 40g (1½oz) butter, melted
- 4 tbsp breadcrumbs (see page 25)
- a handful of chopped fresh herbs, such as parsley, rosemary, and dill
- zest of ½ orange

EQUIPMENT
- lemon zester
- baking tray
- pastry brush
- small bowl
- oven gloves
- fish slice

1 Turn the oven on to 220°C/425°F/gas mark 7.

2 Pour the oil into a baking tray and use a pastry brush to spread it all over – this helps to stop the fish sticking to the tray. Wash the fish.

3 Put the fish on the baking tray and season with a pinch of salt and pepper. **A** Brush each fillet with melted butter.

4 Put the breadcrumbs in a small bowl. Using your fingers, mix in the herbs, orange zest, and a pinch of salt and pepper. **B** Sprinkle the breadcrumbs evenly over the fish fillets.

5 Using oven gloves, put the baking tray in the oven and roast for 10–12 minutes. The fish should be firm and it should have turned from almost see-through to not see-through. (If your fish fillets are 5cm/2 inches thick they will need more than twice as long to cook, i.e. 20–25 minutes.) It is important not to overcook the fish as it will dry out.

6 Using oven gloves, take the tray out of the oven. Use a fish slice to lift the fish off the tray on to four plates. Eat straight away.

roasting fish

A kebab is made up of small pieces of fish, meat or vegetables threaded on to skewers, which are then roasted, grilled, griddled or barbecued. You can use metal skewers or wooden skewers that have been soaked in water to stop them from burning. Fish with a firm, meaty texture, such as cod and monkfish, and oily fish, such as salmon, tuna, swordfish and mackerel, are ideal for kebabs. Fish is often marinated in herbs and spices before being cooked, but it should only be marinated for a short time as its tender flesh absorbs the flavours quickly. If you leave fish in a marinade that contains lots of an acidic ingredient, such as wine or lemon juice, it will start to cook the fish.

cod and crunchy pesto bread kebabs

MAKES 14 SMALL KEBABS (ENOUGH FOR A FAMILY OF 4)

YOU WILL NEED:
INGREDIENTS
- 450g (1lb) cod fillet
- 1 small ciabatta loaf
- 4 tbsp pesto
- 2 tbsp olive oil
- 28 cherry tomatoes
- a little extra oil, for drizzling

EQUIPMENT
- knife
- 2 chopping boards
- serrated knife
- large bowl
- 14 wooden kebab sticks (approx 18cm/7 inches long) soaked in water for at least 30 minutes
- roasting tin
- oven gloves

1 Turn the oven on to 220°C/425°F/gas mark 7.

2 (A) Unless your fish is boneless, run your finger over it to check for bones. If you find any, cut them out with a knife. Cut the fish into 42 x 2.5cm (1 inch) pieces.

3 On another chopping board, use a serrated knife to cut the bread into 42 cubes about the same size as the fish. Put the bread in a bowl and add the pesto and olive oil. (B) Using your hands, mix together so that all the bread is covered in pesto.

4 Take a wooden skewer and thread a piece of fish on to it, then a piece of bread, then a tomato. Continue until there are three pieces each of bread and fish and two tomatoes on each kebab. Lay the kebabs in the roasting tin. Drizzle a little extra oil over the kebabs.

5 Using oven gloves, put the tin in the oven and roast for 10–14 minutes. Using oven gloves, take the tin out of the oven and serve.

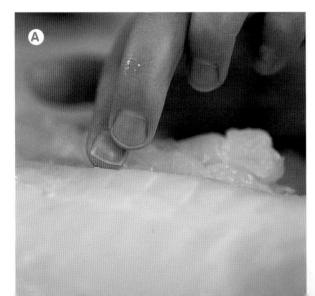

roasting shellfish

There are many types of shellfish, for instance crabs, mussels and prawns. They taste wonderful, but some people find them too fiddly to prepare and eat. You can now buy many types of shellfish from fishmongers or supermarkets ready-prepared, so all the hard work has been done for you. This is my eldest daughter Ella's favourite supper.

roast prawns in garlic butter

SERVES 4

YOU WILL NEED:

INGREDIENTS
- 4 medium potatoes
- 50g (1¾oz) unsalted butter, softened
- 2 large garlic cloves, peeled
- a small handful of fresh parsley, chopped
- a pinch of sea salt and freshly ground black pepper
- 400g (14oz) ready-cooked frozen prawns, defrosted

EQUIPMENT
- vegetable scrubbing brush
- knife
- fork
- oven gloves
- small bowl
- garlic crusher
- metal spoon
- ovenproof dish
- large spoon

1 Turn the oven on to 200°C/400°F/gas mark 6.

2 Use a brush to scrub the potatoes under cold running water. Remove any potato eyes and use a knife to cut out any obvious bad bits or green bits. Use a fork to prick the potatoes a couple of times. Using oven gloves, put the potatoes into the oven to cook for 1 hour.

3 Meanwhile, put the soft butter into a small bowl. Crush the garlic in a garlic crusher and use a metal spoon to mix it into the butter. Add the parsley, salt and pepper, and mix well.

4 Put the prawns into an ovenproof dish and put blobs of garlic butter all over the top.

5 When the potatoes have 7 minutes cooking time left, use oven gloves to put the prawns in the oven.

6 When the potatoes and prawns are cooked, use oven gloves to take them out of the oven.

7 Keeping one oven glove on and holding a knife in your other hand, use the knife to cut a cross in the top of the potato. Push the sides of the potato together to open it up. Repeat with the other potatoes.

8 Put each potato on a serving plate and, using a large spoon, divide the prawns between the potatoes. Serve straight away.

what to find at the sea

The seashore is the place where the sea meets the land. It is the area of land or beach that lies in-between the high tide and low tide marks. At high tide the top of the beach is covered by the sea and when the tide goes out, at low tide, this same land is visible to the eye.

When it is low tide, the upper part of the beach dries out and any pools of water left behind can get very salty. The temperature on the shore and in the water can change quite dramatically – any living plants and animals have to be very adaptable in order to survive.

When you are next on a beach, look for any rock pools. Rock pools are a great place to find living creatures. Each rock pool is likely to have its own community of animals. In the rock pools found in the middle or at the top of the beach you are likely to see a whole variety of seaweed. This provides shade for the animals living underneath it and a place for animals to hide from predators such as seagulls.

Under the seaweed and attached firmly to the rocks you will see limpets, periwinkles, and barnacles. These all have strong shells to protect them from the waves and the drying effect of the wind, and strong muscles to grip the rock. They also have to be tough and strong to help protect them from being bashed off by big crashing waves.

Closer to the sea, limpets can often be found attached to the rocks. I remember my father telling me that if you want to get a limpet away from the rock you need to quickly tap it with a piece of driftwood. If you touch the limpet first it will stick like glue to the rock and will be almost impossible to release. It is also fun to look for periwinkles – you can collect them, but always put them back on the rocks before you go home. You will notice big clusters of mussels attached to the rocks. These are popular cooked with wine, herbs, and garlic in France, although I wouldn't advise cooking mussels found on a beach. Crabs and shrimps survive by hiding in crevices. Buy a cheap fishing net or do as my brothers did and use a piece of netting wrapped around sticks.

On the lower part of the beach – the area nearest the low tide mark – where the beach is wetter you are more likely to find sea anemones, starfish, and seas urchins that all live among the wet seaweeds in the rock pools. You may also be lucky enough to spot some little fish such as blennies. These are not edible, but make a great find.

While you are at the seaside, see if you can find out about any local fishermen and ask them what they have caught that day. You may be in luck and they may offer to sell you some freshly caught fish, which you could cook for your supper.

how to tell if fish is fresh

Just because the fish counter says 'fresh fish for sale', it does not actually guarantee that the fish is 'fresh'. Fish found on some wet-fish counters may have been out of the water for an outrageous two weeks. It could have been chilled on a trawler for a week and then spent a number of days in distribution. Fish that has been kept for this long will not harm you, as long as it has been kept chilled, but neither will it taste that great.

However, there are many fishmongers who take real pride in how quickly they can get fresh fish from sea to shop. When you next go to choose fish, take a long look at it before you buy. To help you decide whether it is fresh and whether it will taste good, think about the following. Whatever happens, don't be shy or embarrassed about taking a good look or asking your fishmonger questions; if he is proud of his fish he should not be concerned about your curiosity. The fish should have clear and bright eyes. The gills under the flaps on either side of the head should be bright red, as this indicates the presence of oxygen – gills stay red for up to four days. The flesh should be firm. Touch the fish with your finger – the pressure should not mark the fish and the flesh should spring back to normal. The skin should look slimy and feel slippery. The fish should have a healthy sea smell, not an ammonia smell, which is a sign of an old fish.

smoking fish

Smoking is a way of preserving food, so that it can be kept for longer without going off – although, of course, it still needs to be used before the 'use-by' date on the pack. Smoked fish also takes on a lovely smoky flavour. Smoked haddock and cod need to be cooked before you can eat them, but some smoked fish, such as smoked salmon, can be very thinly sliced and eaten as they are.

smoked haddock kedgeree

SERVES 4

YOU WILL NEED:

INGREDIENTS
- 450g (1lb) undyed boneless smoked haddock fillets
- 250ml (9fl oz) full-fat milk
- 200ml (7fl oz) cold water
- 200g (7oz) long-grain rice
- 3 hard-boiled eggs (see page 50)
- 40g (1½oz) butter
- a handful of fresh parsley, chopped
- a pinch of salt and freshly ground black pepper

EQUIPMENT
- shallow saucepan or deep frying pan
- medium saucepan
- colander
- slotted spoon
- plate
- knife
- large frying pan
- wooden spoon

1 Wash the fish, put it in a shallow saucepan or deep frying pan and pour over the milk and cold water. Slowly bring to the boil, watching all the time because milk can boil over very quickly. As soon as it bubbles, turn the heat down and cook the fish gently for 8–10 minutes (see page 24), until cooked. Remove from the heat.

2 Fill a medium saucepan three-quarters full with cold water. Bring to the boil, add the rice, and cook for 12 minutes. Take the pan to the sink and drain the rice in a colander.

3 Lift the fish out of the pan using a slotted spoon and put on a plate. Flake the fish into big pieces using your fingers, removing any bits of skin. You can discard the poaching liquid.

4 Peel the eggs and cut each one into eight wedges. Melt the butter in a large frying pan. Add the rice, fish, eggs, and parsley. Stir gently with a wooden spoon over a medium heat until heated through. Taste and add a pinch of salt and pepper. Serve immediately.

poaching fish

Poaching is one of the best ways to cook fish because it cooks food gently and keeps the delicate flesh moist. The fish is placed in a pan, covered with liquid, and cooked over a very low heat or in a very low oven. Poaching is also healthy, as you don't need to use any fat. There are several liquids you can use to poach fish: wine or cider, milk or a mixture of milk and water, or fish or vegetable stock. Whichever is used, it is often flavoured by adding herbs, finely sliced vegetables, such as onions or carrots, lemon juice and spices, such as bay leaves and peppercorns.

White fish, such as cod and haddock, is often poached in milk. The milk can then be used to flavour a sauce, which can make up part of the finished dish. For example, you can strain the poaching liquid and use it to make a white sauce with finely chopped parsley, which you can serve with fish cakes or as the base for a fish pie.

Smoked fish, such as smoked haddock, is often poached in a mixture of milk and water – for example for kedgeree (see page 22). This helps to reduce the smokiness, which can otherwise be a bit overpowering.

Some fish, such as trout or salmon, are delicious poached whole as this keeps the flesh moist, and they are then good served cold. A whole cleaned, scaled, and gutted fish is put in a large pan and covered in water or fish stock. Often vegetables are added to give a subtle flavour to the fish. It is cooked gently, the liquid barely simmering, and is then left to go cold in the liquid. Cold poached fish is often served with a flavoured mayonnaise or other sauce.

Plain fillets, such as plaice or sole, are sometimes poached in wine or cider and served with a creamy sauce made with some of the poaching liquid.

to poach a piece of fish for a pie or fish cakes:

1 Run your fingers over the fish fillet to check for bones (unless you are using a boneless fillet). If you find any, cut them out with a knife. Wash the fish and put it skin-side down into a shallow saucepan or deep frying pan.

2 Pour over enough poaching liquid to cover the fish and add any herbs you are using, such as bay leaves or parsley stalks, to the pan.

3 Ⓐ Very slowly bring up to simmering point, watching carefully, especially if you are using milk.

4 As soon as the liquid bubbles, turn the heat down and cook the fish very gently for 5 minutes – the surface should be wobbling rather than bubbling. If the fish is very thick, you may need to cook it for a minute or 2 longer. When the fish is cooked, the flesh turns from almost see-through to a much denser colour and will feel firmer.

5 Remove from the heat and leave to cool. Lift the fish out of the pan on to a plate using a fish slice. Flake the fish into big pieces using your fingers, removing any bits of skin or bones.

breadcrumbing fish

Fish is often coated in breadcrumbs before cooking, especially if it is going to be shallow-fried or deep-fried. Breadcrumbs protect the fish's delicate flesh from the high heat, seal in the juices, and help to prevent over-cooking. The coating also gives the fish a crispy outer layer, which is a great contrast to the soft fish inside.

When fish is breadcrumbed the crumbs should always be stale and/or dried out in the oven. Dry crumbs will not spit when they go into hot fat and they will absorb less fat than fresh crumbs, making the coating crispier. If you are pan-frying, your fish will only need a very thin layer of breadcrumb coating, but if you are shallow-frying or deep-frying the fish needs to be completely sealed.

To coat the fish, spread some flour mixed with a pinch of salt and pepper on a plate or in a shallow bowl and put some breadcrumbs on another plate. Beat an egg in a shallow bowl. Pat your fish dry on kitchen towel. **A** Dip the fish into the flour and shake off any excess. **B** Then dip it into the egg and let the excess drip off. Then dip it into the breadcrumbs, turning it over and using your other hand to sprinkle crumbs over the fish so that it is covered. Lay it on a plate ready to cook.

Breadcrumbs store well either in an airtight container or in a sealed container in the freezer.

to make breadcrumbs:

1 Tear the bread into small pieces. Whiz them in a food processor until you have fine breadcrumbs – you may need to stop the processor and push down any large bits of bread that have got stuck around the blade, but be careful as the blade is very sharp. Whiz again until the crumbs are fine and there are no big lumps.

2 Carefully remove the blade and tip the crumbs out into a bowl. If you need fresh breadcrumbs, to put into stuffing for example, this is all you need to do.

3 If you are breadcrumbing fish, turn the oven on to 150°C/300°F/gas mark 2. Spread the crumbs out evenly in a roasting tin. Using oven gloves, put the tray into the oven and cook for 10 minutes. Using oven gloves, remove from the oven and mix the crumbs around with a wooden spoon so they dry out evenly. Put them back in the oven for another 10 minutes. They should be crisp and a very pale gold when they are done. Cool then store in an airtight container.

breadcrumbing fish

Making fish cakes is a great way to use lots of simple techniques you have already learnt: boiling and mashing potatoes, poaching fish, breadcrumbing, and frying.

cod fish cakes

MAKES 8 SMALL FISH CAKES

YOU WILL NEED:

INGREDIENTS
- 450g (1lb) old potatoes, peeled and cut into quarters
- 45g (1½oz) butter
- 500ml (18fl oz) full-fat milk
- 400g (14oz) boneless cod fillets, skinned
- a large handful of fresh parsley, chopped
- a large pinch of sea salt and freshly ground black pepper
- 50g (1¾oz) plain flour
- 100g (3½oz) fine breadcrumbs (see page 25)
- 2 eggs
- a little oil, for frying
- lemon wedges, to serve

EQUIPMENT
- vegetable peeler
- knife
- chopping board
- 2 medium saucepans
- colander and potato masher
- fish slice
- 5 plates
- wooden spoon
- shallow bowl and fork
- frying pan and kitchen paper

GOOD THINGS TO ADD TO YOUR FISH CAKES
- ✔ 1–2 tbsp pesto or tomato ketchup
- ✔ chopped herbs, such as basil or coriander
- ✔ chopped olives or capers
- ✔ different fish: if you are short on time try using tinned tuna or chopped cooked prawns, if you like a smoky flavour use poached smoked haddock

1 Boil the potatoes in a saucepan until tender. Drain in a colander and mash with 20g (¾oz) of the butter and 3 tbsp of the milk (see page 96).

2 Wash the fish and put it into a saucepan. Pour over the remaining milk, then slowly bring to simmering point, watching all the time. As soon as it bubbles, turn the heat down and cook the fish gently for 5 minutes until cooked – if the fish is very thick you may need to cook it for a minute longer (see page 24, point 4).

3 Remove from the heat and leave to cool. Using a fish slice, lift the fish out of the pan and put it on a plate. Flake the fish into big pieces using your fingers, removing any bits of skin.

4 Mix the fish into the mashed potato and stir in the parsley and a pinch of salt and pepper.

5 Put the flour on to a plate and mix in a pinch of salt and pepper. Put the breadcrumbs on to another plate. Crack the eggs into a shallow bowl and beat well with a fork.

6 Wash and dry your hands well. Divide the potato mixture into 8 portions and roll each one into a ball. Flatten each portion gently into a round fish cake.

7 Turn each fish cake in the flour to coat, then dip in the beaten eggs and then in the breadcrumbs, making sure they are completely covered (see page 25). Lay the fish cakes on a clean plate ready to cook while you finish coating the rest. Wash your hands.

8 Melt the remaining butter with the oil in a frying pan and heat until the butter starts to bubble. Add 4 fish cakes and cook for 2–3 minutes. Use a fish slice to turn the fish cakes over, and cook on the other side for another 2–3 minutes. Remove from the pan and keep warm on a plate lined with kitchen paper while you cook the rest.

2 FROM THE FARM

cutting meat

Knowing how to cut meat is an important skill. Make sure you use a sharp knife; there is more chance of the knife slipping if you use a blunt one. Always cut meat on a wooden or plastic surface and hold the knife firmly, with the blade pointing away from you. Cut away from your hands and body so that if the knife does slip you won't cut yourself. All cuts of meat are different. Some, such as chicken breasts, are fairly easy to cut. Others, such as stewing steak, are tougher and can be hard to chop. If you do come across bone or sinew, don't force it; just try cutting in a different place.

crispy Mexican chicken nuggets

SERVES 4

YOU WILL NEED:
INGREDIENTS
- 55g (2oz) softened butter, plus a small piece for greasing tin
- 1 garlic clove, peeled and crushed
- 55g (2oz) barbecue sauce
- pinch of freshly ground black pepper
- 150g (5½oz) lightly salted plain tortilla chips
- 3 boneless skinless chicken breasts
- a little oil, for greasing

EQUIPMENT
- large roasting tin
- small bowl
- small wooden spoon
- garlic crusher
- plastic sandwich bag
- rolling pin
- large plate
- chopping board
- 2 knives
- kitchen paper
- oven gloves

1 Turn the oven on to 180°C/350°F/gas mark 4. Rub a little butter on to a large roasting tin. Put the 55g (2oz) of butter into a small bowl and beat well with a wooden spoon until soft. Beat in the crushed garlic, barbecue sauce and pepper.

2 Put the tortilla chips into a plastic sandwich bag, seal and bash with a rolling pin. When the chips are crushed, tip them out on to a large plate.

3 Put the chicken breasts on to a chopping board (for hygiene, keep one board for chopping meat and fish and a different board for fruit and vegetables – never cut raw and cooked food on the same board). **A** Using a knife, cut each breast in half lengthways and then cut each half into thin strips.

4 Lay the strips of chicken on kitchen paper and pat them dry. Mix the chicken in with the butter until the chicken is covered.

5 **B** Dip a few buttery strips of chicken into the crushed chips. Turn each strip over, pressing down so the chicken is evenly coated in chips. Lay the coated chicken in the roasting tin in a single layer. Repeat with the remaining strips of chicken. Sprinkle any remaining chips over the chicken. Wash your hands.

6 Using oven gloves, put the roasting tin into the oven. Cook the chicken for 8–10 minutes. Use oven gloves to remove the tin from the oven, chop open the biggest nugget with a clean knife to check it is cooked: the meat should be a solid white colour (not at all translucent), with no traces of pink; if not put it back in the oven for a couple of minutes.

kebabs

Kebabs are small pieces of meat, usually beef or lamb, sometimes chicken, fish or vegetables, threaded on to wooden or metal skewers and grilled, griddled or roasted. They were originally cooked in Turkey, became popular throughout the Middle East, and are now eaten all over the world. Anything cooked on a skewer like this can be called a kebab, even fruit! You can use either wooden or metal skewers, but if you use wooden skewers you will need to soak them in water for at least half an hour first to stop them from burning.

There are two main types of kebab: shish and doner. Shish kebabs are traditionally made from lamb or mutton, marinated (see below) in yoghurt, oil and spices, and cooked over hot embers or coals. Sometimes they are served on the skewers, and sometimes they are taken off on to a bed of rice or couscous or into pitta bread. Doner kebabs are made from slices of meat threaded on to a large skewer or spit, which is turned constantly, over several hours, so that the meat cooks evenly. The meat is then sliced off in long thin pieces and served in pitta bread with salad and yoghurt.

The ingredients for kebabs need a firm texture so they do not fall apart during cooking. When preparing a kebab, you will need to cut all the pieces the same size so that they cook evenly.

marinades

It is a good idea to marinate the kebab ingredients before you grill them. A marinade is a liquid that is flavoured with herbs or spices. It may contain oil, lemon juice, vinegar, wine or yoghurt. Food, usually meat, fish or vegetables, is soaked in this liquid for an hour, overnight, or sometimes for longer. This process is called marinating. Its purpose is to give flavour to the food, but also to make it more tender and keep it moist during cooking. For example, try mixing 2 tablespoons of soy sauce with 2 tablespoons of runny honey, the juice of half a lemon and a peeled and crushed garlic clove. This is perfect for chicken or pork. Or mix 1 tablespoon of lemon juice with 2 tablespoons of olive oil and a peeled and crushed garlic clove for a marinade for prawns.

For kebabs made from fruit, such as banana and pineapple, try drizzling over honey or brushing with butter and then sieving over a little icing sugar and grilling until the sugar starts to caramelise.

making the kebabs

If you are making a kebab that combines meat and vegetables, it is a good idea to alternate the ingredients. **A** For example, to make the Thai chicken kebabs on page 33, thread a piece of chicken on to the skewer, then add a piece of pepper, then another piece of chicken, and so on until the skewer is full. **B** Continue threading on to skewers in this way until you have no ingredients left.

cooking the kebabs

There are a few ways to cook kebabs: put the food under a hot grill, on a barbecue, on a griddle pan or in a hot oven. I prefer to griddle kebabs, as the food cooks quickly and the direct contact with the hot griddle pan gives the food a lovely, slightly charred flavour, and helps to seal the juices inside the food.

kebabs

Marinating is a great technique, especially if you like cooking meat and fish. Marinades add a subtle flavour to the food, and adding lemon or lime juice will help to make the meat or fish really tender and juicy (see page 31). Satay sauce is made with peanuts, sometimes with added spices.

Thai chicken kebabs with satay sauce

SERVES 4

YOU WILL NEED:
INGREDIENTS
• juice of 1 lime
• 2 tsp Thai red curry paste
• 100ml (3½fl oz) coconut milk
• 3 boneless skinless chicken breasts
• 1 red pepper

for the satay sauce:
• 150ml (5½fl oz) coconut milk
• ½ level tsp Thai red curry paste
• 125g (4½oz) crunchy peanut butter with no added salt
• 1 tsp brown sugar

EQUIPMENT
• small saucepan
• large shallow bowl
• small whisk
• 2 chopping boards
• 2 knives
• metal skewers or wooden kebab sticks, soaked in water for at least half an hour
• clingfilm
• wooden spoon
• roasting tin
• oven gloves

1 Put 1 tablespoon of the lime juice into a small saucepan and put to one side for the peanut sauce. Put the red curry paste, coconut milk and the rest of the lime juice into a large shallow bowl, then whisk together.

2 Put the chicken on a chopping board. Using a knife, cut the chicken into 1cm (½ inch) cubes.

3 Put the pepper on a separate chopping board, cut in half and remove the seeds. Cut it into the same sized pieces as the chicken.

4 Make the chicken kebabs (see page 31). Put all the kebabs into the bowl with the coconut milk marinade. Push them down and turn them over so they are covered in the mixture. Cover the bowl with clingfilm and leave to marinate in the refrigerator for at least an hour.

5 To make the satay sauce, pour the coconut milk into the small saucepan with the lime juice, and add the curry paste and peanut butter. Heat gently, stirring often with a wooden spoon, until the sauce is smooth and hot – this will take about 5 minutes.

6 Turn the oven on to 180°C/350°F/gas mark 4.

7 Take the kebabs out of the marinade and lay them in a roasting tin. Pour over half the remaining marinade. Using oven gloves, put the tin in the preheated oven and cook for 10–15 minutes, until the kebabs are crispy and sticky and the chicken is cooked (see page 30, point 7). Using oven gloves, take the tin out of the oven. Reheat the satay sauce gently and serve with the kebabs.

using mince

Mince tends to be made from beef or lamb, although some recipes call for pork mince. Beef mince is usually made from the meat left on the carcass, mainly from around the neck and shoulder, and sometimes the shin or brisket. It is used in a variety of ways, including in beef burgers, bolognese sauce and chilli con carne. Lamb mince is ideal for dishes such as moussaka and shepherd's pie, where middle neck, scrag end and the leaner parts of the belly are often minced. Pork mince tends to be made from the hind quarters and can be used in dishes such as meatballs. The mince that you find in the supermarkets can be very finely ground and, when it is cooked, all the juices run out of it and it becomes insipid. If you buy mince from a butcher you can ask for it to be minced a little coarser.

beef burgers

MAKES 8 SMALL BURGERS

Mince for a burger should have some fat in it, as this will make your burger lovely and juicy. Minced rump steak is delicious but expensive. Minced chuck or blade steak is also good.

YOU WILL NEED:

INGREDIENTS
- 2 spring onions
- 500g (1lb 2oz) good-quality beef mince
- a pinch of salt and freshly ground black pepper
- 1 small garlic clove, peeled
- 8 burger buns or bread rolls
- 8 crunchy lettuce leaves, such as iceberg, little gem or cos
- 1 large beef tomato, sliced
- ketchup and mayonnaise, to serve

EQUIPMENT
- chopping board
- knife
- large bowl and plate
- garlic crusher
- grill pan
- kitchen tongs

1 On a chopping board, use a knife to chop the hairy root end and the very dark leaves off the spring onions. Cut the trimmed onions up as finely as you can. Put them into a large bowl.

2 Add the beef mince, salt and pepper to the bowl. **A** Crush the garlic in the garlic crusher and add that too. Mix everything together with your hands.

3 Take a quarter of the mixture and divide it in two. **B** Use your hands to roll each bit into a ball, then pat it flat into a burger shape and put on to a plate. Repeat with the rest of the mixture so you have 8 burgers.

4 Turn the grill on to high. Put the burgers on to the grill pan and cook for about 6 minutes, then use the tongs to carefully turn them over and cook for another 6 minutes. To check that the burgers are cooked all the way through, cut the biggest one in half – if it looks pink in the middle, put all of the burger back under the grill for a few more minutes.

5 Cut the buns in half across the middle and put a piece of lettuce on the bottom and a slice of tomato on top of it. Put a burger on top, add a little ketchup or mayonnaise and put the top half of the bun on top of that.

how stock is raised for food

Nearly all the food that we eat every day comes from farms. Farming means using land to rear animals and to grow crops to provide food for people to eat. Farming began when, instead of hunting animals, people started to gather wild goats and sheep into herds.

Long ago, these herds were moved from one place to another to find fresh areas for grazing. It was only when people started to grow crops for their own food and animals that real farming began. People stayed in one area and developed the land around them, relying on the crops and animals for food to feed themselves and their families. As they became more skilful at farming they could grow more than they needed. This surplus food could be exchanged for other foods, such as sugar, or cloth.

Gradually farming became more and more sophisticated, with a whole variety of machinery and tools introduced to make life easier and more efficient for farmers. In the last fifty or so years the use of chemicals in the form of pesticides and fertilizers, and the use of genetically modified crops (GM), has revolutionised farming.

The most extreme type of this is intensive farming, where hedges are destroyed and large areas of land are made into enormous fields. There is growing concern that this way of farming is not good for the environment or for us. More and more farmers are trying to return to old-fashioned methods of farming, where stock and crops are raised naturally and humanely, with respect for the world in which we live.

sheep

Sheep are kept for their wool, meat and milk. Lamb is meat from young animals and mutton from slightly older animals. Mutton can actually be meat from any lamb over one year old. You will probably be most familiar with eating lamb mince, lamb chops and legs of lamb that are often roasted for Sunday dinner.

cattle

Cattle can be kept for milk (dairy cows), which is sold for drinking or made into dairy products, such as cheese, yoghurt and butter. Alternatively they can be reared for meat (beef cattle). Although it is rare for cattle to be raised for both meat and milk, dairy cows can be sold for meat. A variety of different cuts of meat come from cows, including fillet and rump steaks and stewing steak, which is perfect for slow cooking to make stews and casseroles. Also some of the meat, mainly from around the neck and shoulder, is made into mince (used in recipes like beef burgers).

pigs

Pigs are also kept for their meat. Some farms raise pigs indoors in big sheds, which are often just like battery hen farms (see page 49) but for pigs. Pigs raised outside are tough outdoor breeds, which produce very good meat. It is much nicer for pigs to be raised outdoors, where they can wallow in mud to cool down and root with their snouts in the ground for things like acorns. Pigs are very sociable animals and like to be around other pigs. Some of the most popular foods from pigs are sausages, pork chops and bacon.

chickens

As with hens kept for their eggs, many chickens reared for meat are subjected to a poor quality of life. They can be crammed into sheds with artificial light, fed a high protein diet and routinely given antibiotics. Free-range chickens, however, are given the chance to roam around outside, nibbling at worms and scratching the ground. It is important to remember that the eating quality of any bird depends on three factors: the breed, a wholesome diet, and being allowed to roam outside. Roasting the whole bird is very popular, and it can be seasoned with butter and herbs to make it particularly tasty (see page 44). Chicken breasts are popular cuts of the bird, as are chicken thighs and drumsticks.

frying meat

There are two ways to fry meat. One way is to cook it so that you can eat it straight away – for example, frying a steak or lamb fillet. The meat is fried over a medium or high heat, often with little or no oil because as the meat is cooked the fat it contains is released. This method of frying is often called 'sautéing'.

The second way to fry meat is to give flavour and colour to a dish. The meat is fried quickly in oil, in a large heavy-based pan over a high heat, until the outside is golden. The inside may not necessarily be cooked through, as the cooking will be finished later. For example, you may fry cubes of beef or lamb, and then finish the cooking in a stew or casserole. This method of frying is often called 'browning'.

spaghetti carbonara

SERVES 4

YOU WILL NEED:

INGREDIENTS
- 2 whole eggs
- 2 egg yolks
- 6 tbsp double cream
- 55g (2oz) Parmesan, finely grated
- a large pinch of sea salt and freshly ground black pepper
- 200g (7oz) streaky bacon or cubes of pancetta (Italian bacon)
- 1 tbsp olive oil
- 450g (1lb) spaghetti

EQUIPMENT
- jug
- fork
- kitchen scissors
- frying pan
- long-handled wooden spoon
- large saucepan with lid
- oven gloves
- colander

1 Crack an egg into a jug by tapping the egg firmly against the side of the jug, pushing your thumbs into the crack and carefully pulling the shell apart, letting the egg drop into the jug. Repeat with the second egg. Add the yolks, cream, cheese and a pinch of salt and pepper and whisk with a fork.

2 Using scissors, snip the bacon into small pieces. Heat the oil in a frying pan, add the bacon, turn the heat up a little, and leave to cook for 2 minutes. (A) Turn the bacon over carefully, stirring occasionally with the wooden spoon. Cook for about 5 minutes. Remove the pan from the heat.

3 Three-quarters fill a large saucepan with water. Add a large pinch of salt, cover with a lid and bring to the boil. Carefully put the spaghetti into the pan, wait a moment for it to soften, then use the long-handled wooden spoon to push it down into the water.

4 Bring back to the boil, turn down to a simmer and cook according to the packet instructions (see page 125, points 4–6). When the pasta is cooked, use oven gloves to take the pan to the sink and drain the pasta in a colander (the pan may be heavy, so ask an adult for help with this). Tip the pasta back into the pan and add the cooked bacon. Return the pan to the hob and cook over a low heat for 1 minute, stirring well with the wooden spoon.

5 Pour over the egg mixture and stir constantly for 1 minute. Remove the pan from the heat and continue to stir for 2–3 minutes. The heat from the saucepan and pasta will cook the eggs. Serve straight away.

frying meat

'Hot dog' may seem like a funny name for a sausage in a bun, but when you look at its history it all makes sense. German immigrants to America started selling sausages in buns from street carts in New York as long ago as the 1860s. In Germany they were often called 'little dogs', as they looked a little bit like dachshunds or sausage dogs. The snack became more and more popular and the Americans started to call them 'hot dogs'.

mini hot dogs

MAKES 4

YOU WILL NEED:
INGREDIENTS
- 1 red onion
- 2 tbsp olive oil
- 4 good-quality pork sausages
- 1 medium French stick or baguette
- ketchup or mustard, to serve

EQUIPMENT
- 2 chopping boards
- knife
- frying pan
- wooden spoon
- slotted spoon
- plate
- kitchen foil
- kitchen tongs
- fork
- bread board
- bread knife

1 Put the onion on a chopping board and, using a knife, cut it in half. Peel the onion, then slice it as thinly as you can (see page 100).

2 Heat the oil in a frying pan, add the onion and cook for 5 minutes, until soft, stirring with a wooden spoon. Using a slotted spoon, lift the onion on to a plate and cover with foil to keep it warm.

3 Put the frying pan back over a medium heat. Add the sausages and fry for 10 minutes, turning often until they are golden brown all over. Take the pan off the heat.

4 Using tongs, put the sausages on to a clean chopping board. Hold a sausage steady with a fork (they will be very hot) and, using a knife, cut the sausage in half lengthways. Repeat with the other sausages.

5 Put the sausages, cut-side down, back in the frying pan and cook them over a medium heat for 1–2 more minutes, until cooked. Take the pan off the heat.

6 Using a bread board and a bread knife, cut the French stick into 4 equal pieces a little shorter than a sausage. Carefully cut each piece in half lengthways, but do not to cut all the way through the bread.

7 Open out each slice of French bread by pressing on it lightly. Divide the onion between the 4 pieces. Rest 2 halves of sausage in each one, letting a bit stick out on either side of the bread so that they look like long sausages. Top each one with a good squirt of ketchup or mustard.

grilling meat

Grilled meat is cooked quickly, and often gets a charred surface, which gives it a great flavour. To ensure this happens, the grill must be preheated to its highest setting – this may take around 10 minutes.

Because grilling does not make meat more tender, as stewing or slow-roasting does, only tender cuts of meat should be grilled. For example, sirloin steaks, burgers made from good-quality mince, chicken breasts and pork or lamb chops are all fine for grilling.

It is often good to marinate meat before grilling (see page 31), because this helps keep it moist under the high heat. Never add salt to meat before you grill it, because the salt will draw out the juices that you are trying to keep inside. Also, never overcook the meat or it may become dry.

simple lamb chops

SERVES 4

YOU WILL NEED:
INGREDIENTS
- 1 tbsp olive oil
- 4 tsp mint jelly
- 4 lamb chops
- few rosemary sprigs

EQUIPMENT
- grill pan
- kitchen foil and pastry brush
- small bowl
- oven gloves
- kitchen tongs and skewer

COOKING TIMES
Approx times for grilling meat under a high heat:
- steak, 2.5cm(1 inch) thick – approx 1½-2 minutes each side for rare; 3 minutes each side for medium; 4 minutes each side for well done
- pork chops – approx 10 minutes each side, depending on size
- lamb chops – approx 10 minutes each side, depending on size
- lamb cutlets – approx 5 minutes each side, depending on size

1 Turn the grill on to its highest setting – it may take up to 10 minutes to get really hot. This is important, as you want to cook the outside of the meat as quickly as possible to keep the inside tender and juicy.

2 Line a grill pan with kitchen foil and use a pastry brush to brush a little oil all over the foil.

3 Put the mint jelly into a small bowl. **(A)** Brush the chops with oil and put them on to the grill pan. Brush the mint jelly over the lamb chops and scatter over a few rosemary sprigs.

4 **(B)** Using oven gloves, put the grill pan under the heat, ideally so that the meat is about 5–7.5cm (2–3 inches) away from the heat.

5 Grill for 10 minutes, then use oven gloves to take the grill pan out of the oven and turn the chops over using tongs. Cook for another 10 minutes.

6 To test if the lamb is cooked, push a skewer into the thickest part of the meat to see if the juices are the right colour. Pink juices indicate blood, which tells you that the meat is not cooked through. If you are grilling lamb or beef you may like the meat to be slightly rare in the middle, but pork should always be cooked right through.

roasting meat

Oven-roasting means cooking meat in the oven with a little fat – for example, drizzled with some olive oil or rubbed with butter. The great thing about roasting is that, although it takes a while, you don't have to do much while the meat is cooking. You may need to baste the meat (spoon the cooking juices over it to stop it from drying out) halfway through cooking.

   The best meats to roast are the ones between tender and tough – for example, a leg of lamb, a whole chicken, a belly of pork or a rib of beef. Ideally you want meat on the bone, which will give it a very good flavour.

roast chicken

SERVES 4–6

There are two main ways of roasting a chicken: fast at a high temperature, or slow at a lower temperature. If you're cooking the bird slowly, it needs to be regularly basted. I prefer the quicker method, as the chicken stays moist, and it is simple to do.

YOU WILL NEED:

INGREDIENTS
- 25g (1oz) softened butter, plus a small piece for greasing tin
- 2 tbsp chopped fresh herbs, such as tarragon, rosemary or parsley
- 1 chicken approx 1.3kg (3lb)
- 1 onion, peeled
- a pinch each of salt and freshly ground black pepper
- 3 rashers streaky bacon

for the gravy:
- 1 tbsp plain flour
- 300ml (10fl oz) good chicken or vegetable stock or vegetable water

EQUIPMENT
- roasting tin
- small bowl
- metal spoon
- large plate
- knife
- chopping board
- oven gloves
- skewer
- 2 fish slices
- serving dish
- kitchen foil
- wooden spoon

1   Take the chicken out of the refrigerator about 30 minutes before you need to cook it. Turn the oven on to 230°C/450°F/gas mark 8. Rub the base and sides of the roasting tin with a little butter.

2   Put the 25g (1oz) of butter and the herbs into a small bowl and use your hand or a metal spoon to mix well. Put the chicken on a large plate and remove any string. Using clean hands, rub half of the herb butter inside the cavity of the chicken and the other half over the outside, using your fingers to push some of the butter under the skin of the breasts without tearing the skin.

3   Using a knife and a chopping board, cut the onion into 8 wedges and push these into the cavity of the chicken. Season with salt and pepper and place the bacon rashers across the breast. Place in the roasting tin and, using oven gloves, put the tin in the oven. Roast for 50 minutes then, using oven gloves, bring the tin out of the oven.

4   There are two ways to check if the chicken is cooked. Push a skewer into the thickest part of the leg, take it out and press it flat against the flesh to see if the juices run clear. Alternatively give the leg a tug – if it comes away from the body easily the chicken is cooked. You may need to cook the chicken for another 10 minutes otherwise.

5   Using 2 fish slices, lift the chicken on to a warm serving dish. Cover with foil and leave to rest for 15 minutes, so the juices run back into the meat, keeping it all juicy and moist.

6   To make the gravy, slowly pour most of the fat out of the roasting tin, trying to keep as much of the juice as possible. Put the tin on to the hob and heat the fat over a medium heat. Add the flour and, using a wooden spoon, stir for 1 minute. Add the stock or vegetable water and stir until the sauce boils – 3–4 minutes. Simmer for 3 minutes. Add a pinch of salt and pepper.

3 FROM THE DAIRY

Eggs

Traditionally, most farms and many families kept hens. It was much more economical than buying eggs because hens are relatively easy to keep and can be fed with kitchen scraps, such as vegetable peelings and bacon rind.

In this way most people, even those without much space, were able to have lovely fresh eggs every day.

Hens reared in this old-fashioned way are allowed to roam outside all day, scratching in the dirt, looking for worms, grains and bugs to eat. In case you were wondering, hens are not vegetarian!

Even on a big farm where hens can wander freely, they will not fly away or roam too far, they always stay near to their nests. When it

starts to get dark the hens naturally head back to the hen house where they roost for the night. The hen house must be shut to keep the hens safe from predators such as foxes. First thing in the morning the door is opened so that the hens can come back out.

A healthy hen will lay between 180 and 320 eggs per year. The amount can vary between hens depending on their breed, age, diet, and even the time of year – hens tend to lay more in the summer. The hen will usually come out of the hen house and cluck loudly after she has laid an egg.

Fewer people keep hens in this way today because eggs are so widely available in supermarkets and they are very cheap. But people are gradually beginning to realise that keeping hens can be fun and the eggs from your own hens often taste much better because of their varied diet. Hens reared at home, or on smaller chicken farms, often have a much nicer life than hens from enormous battery farms.

It can appear to be easy to keep hens and, once you are set up with two or three hens, a hen house and a big run, you will probably only need to spend 10 minutes a day feeding them and letting them into (and bringing them back in from) the garden. But if you are keen to keep hens, contact your Environmental Health Officer to see if there are any reasons why you should not keep poultry in your area. Also, don't forget to speak to your neighbours.

battery farms

Of all eggs on sale today in the UK approximately eighty-eight per cent are laid by hens kept in battery cages.

Battery houses are big sheds, which often have no windows, so they have little natural light or fresh air. Each shed can hold 30,000–100,000 hens. To fit this number of hens into one shed each hen is kept in a little cage. When the hen lays an egg it rolls down into a tray, where it is collected. All the hen cages are piled on top of each other – it is like a prison for hens.

barn eggs

Barn hens are kept in a similar way to battery hens, although they are allowed to roam all over the barn rather than being kept in a cage. However, barns can be just as crowded as a battery farm.

free-range eggs

Free-range hens can go outside, but their outside space is limited, although it does vary from farm to farm. They get some daylight and can peck and scratch the ground like they would naturally. Generally, the smaller free-range egg producers look after their hens well.

organic eggs

Organic hens are usually kept in smaller flocks and generally they have more space. They also have easy access to outside areas where they can roam over organic land and they are fed organic feed.

We tend to use the word 'chicken' to describe the meat we eat from a hen. A flock of the birds can be called hens or chickens, but a girl chicken is a hen and a boy chicken is a cockerel (or rooster in the USA). In the UK alone we each eat about 170 eggs each a year. Egg shells can be white or brown, but there is no difference in the taste. The shell's colour is determined by the breed of hen that laid it. There are lots of breeds of chickens, some have amazing coloured feathers and plumage, especially cockerels.

boiling eggs

Boiling eggs is simple, so once you have mastered the art, boiled egg and soldiers makes a fun and easy meal. Be sure to use fresh free-range eggs that are well within their 'use-by' date and avoid giving uncooked eggs to very small children.

boiled egg and soldiers

SERVES 1

YOU WILL NEED:

INGREDIENTS
- 1 medium egg
- 1 slice of bread
- a knob of butter

EQUIPMENT
- saucepan
- long-handled slotted spoon
- egg timer or watch
- egg cup
- spoon
- toaster
- chopping board
- knife

1 If your egg has been kept in the refrigerator, it will need to warm up before you boil it, so put it into a saucepan with cold water and bring to the boil.

2 If your egg has been kept out of the refrigerator, three-quarters fill a saucepan with water and bring to the boil. Lower your egg into the saucepan using a long-handled slotted spoon.

3 As soon as the water comes to the boil, set the timer for 4 minutes. This will give you a soft-boiled egg, with a runny yolk for dipping toast soldiers into. If you prefer a hard-boiled egg with a firm yolk, set the timer for 7 minutes. If you are cooking a large egg, add 1 minute to the cooking time.

4 **A** When your egg is done, lift it out of the pan with the slotted spoon. **B** Put it into an egg cup and leave to cool slightly before you break the top off with a spoon.

5 Pop your bread into the toaster and cook until golden brown. Put it on to a chopping board and spread it with butter. Cut it into 4 long strips.

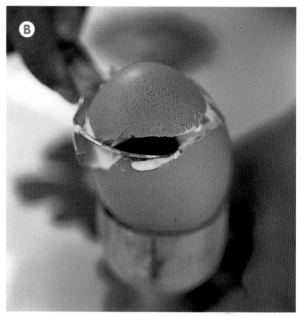

scrambling eggs

If you are making scrambled eggs for a special occasion, maybe for your mum on Mother's Day, add a little cream instead of milk. Scrambled eggs are good served on toast.

SERVES 4

YOU WILL NEED:

INGREDIENTS
- 8 medium eggs
- 6 tbsp full-fat milk (or 3 tbsp each of milk and single cream)
- a pinch of salt and freshly ground black pepper
- a big knob of butter

EQUIPMENT
- medium bowl
- fork
- medium saucepan
- wooden spoon

1 Crack an egg into a medium bowl by tapping the egg firmly against the side of the bowl, pushing your thumbs into the crack, and carefully pulling the shell apart, letting the egg drop into the bowl. Repeat with the remaining eggs.

2 Add the milk and/or cream and salt and pepper. **A** Whisk with a fork.

3 Melt the butter in a medium saucepan over a medium heat. Gently tip the pan so that the sides are coated with butter.

4 When the butter just begins to bubble, pour in the beaten eggs.

5 **B** Stir gently with a wooden spoon, moving the mixture all around the pan to prevent the eggs from sticking to the bottom. When all the runny bits of egg have been cooked – this will take 3–4 minutes – take the pan off the heat. Serve straight away.

poaching eggs

When poaching eggs, it is important to use the freshest eggs you can, under four days old if possible, as they will hold their shape well. Adding a little vinegar to the water will also help the eggs hold their shape – but don't worry, you can't taste it! Avoid giving uncooked eggs to very small children.

SERVES 2

YOU WILL NEED:

INGREDIENTS
- 1 tsp vinegar
- 2 eggs

EQUIPMENT
- medium to large frying pan
- jug
- small bowl
- egg timer or watch
- kitchen paper
- plate
- slotted spoon

GOOD THINGS TO EAT WITH POACHED EGGS
- ✔ baked beans
- ✔ grilled bacon
- ✔ salad (see page 109)
- ✔ grilled mushrooms
- ✔ big chips (see page 92)

1   Put a frying pan on the hob, then use a jug to fill it three-quarters full with cold water. Add the vinegar and stir.

2   On a low heat, bring the water just to simmering point. You should be able to see tiny bubbles simmering on the bottom of the pan, but not on the surface of the water.

3   **A** Crack an egg into a small bowl by tapping the egg firmly against the side of the bowl, pushing your thumbs into the crack, and carefully pulling the shell apart, letting the egg drop into the bowl. **B** Carefully tip the egg into the pan. Repeat with the remaining egg and add it to the pan, making sure the eggs are not touching.

4   Set the egg timer for 1 minute, but watch the pan to make sure it doesn't boil. The gently simmering water will set the outside of the egg white, which will prevent the egg from spreading; if it boils the egg white can separate into thin ribbons.

5   Turn the heat off and move the pan to the cool side of the hob. Set the egg timer for 10 minutes – the eggs will continue to cook in the hot water even though the pan is off the heat.

6   Put 2–3 sheets of kitchen paper on to a plate. Put the pan next to the plate. Use a slotted spoon to lift an egg on to the paper to drain. Repeat with the other egg. Serve straight away.

poaching eggs

This salad has a lovely combination of textures: soft eggs, crunchy croûtons and crisp lettuce. It makes a great summery lunch. Be sure to use fresh free-range eggs that are well within their 'use-by' date and avoid giving uncooked eggs to very small children.

warm poached egg and bacon salad

SERVES 4

YOU WILL NEED:

INGREDIENTS
- 2 thick slices of white bread
- 6 tbsp olive oil
- 8 bacon rashers
- 1 tsp vinegar
- 4 medium eggs
- 1 medium romaine or cos lettuce, washed
- 2 tbsp lemon juice
- 1 tsp balsamic vinegar
- a pinch of soft brown sugar
- a pinch of salt and freshly ground black pepper

EQUIPMENT
- chopping board
- knife
- 3 small bowls
- 2 medium baking trays
- oven gloves
- kitchen scissors
- 5 plates
- medium to large frying pan
- slotted spoon
- kitchen paper
- whisk

1 Turn the oven on to 200°C/400°F/gas mark 6. Put the bread on to a chopping board and, using a knife, cut each slice into strips, then cut each strip into small cubes.

2 For the croûtons, put the bread cubes into a bowl, add 2 tablespoons of the oil and use your hands to mix them around until they are covered in oil.

3 Put the bread cubes on to a baking tray and spread them out evenly. Put the bacon on to a second baking tray.

4 Using oven gloves, put the bacon into the oven on the top shelf and cook for 6 minutes. Put the bread into the oven alongside the bacon and cook for 6–8 minutes.

5 Using oven gloves, take the trays out of the oven. Use scissors to snip the bacon into small pieces and put into a small bowl.

6 Poach the eggs (see page 53).

7 Tear the lettuce leaves into small pieces and divide between 4 plates. Sprinkle over the bacon and croûtons. Put an egg on top of each plate.

8 Put the remaining oil, lemon juice, balsamic vinegar, sugar and salt and pepper into a bowl. Whisk together and then drizzle over the salads. Serve straight away.

omelettes

Omelettes are a little challenging, if only because you have to try and get them out of the frying pan in one piece! But once you've mastered them there are lots of fillings you can add.

cheese omelette

SERVES 1

YOU WILL NEED:

INGREDIENTS
- 40g (1½oz) Cheddar or Gruyère
- 2 medium eggs
- a pinch of salt and freshly ground black pepper
- 1 tbsp cold water
- a knob of butter
- 1 tsp olive oil

EQUIPMENT
- cheese grater
- small plate and medium bowl
- fork
- frying pan
- wooden spoon
- palette knife

GOOD THINGS TO SPRINKLE OVER YOUR OMELETTE
- ✔ different types of grated cheese, such as Red Leicester
- ✔ crumbled blue cheese
- ✔ chopped cooked ham
- ✔ crumbled cooked bacon
- ✔ fried sliced mushrooms
- ✔ a little chopped parsley or tarragon

1 Coarsely grate the cheese on to a plate (see page 69).

2 Crack an egg into a medium bowl by tapping the egg firmly against the side of the bowl, pushing your thumbs into the crack, and carefully pulling the shell apart, letting the egg drop into the bowl. Do the same with the second egg. Add the salt and pepper and then the water – this makes the omelette lighter.

3 Use a fork to gently beat the eggs: don't whisk them, just mix the yolk and white together.

4 Melt the butter and oil together in a frying pan over a medium heat.

5 **A** Turn up the heat and, as soon as the butter starts to foam, pour in the beaten eggs. Quickly tilt the pan so that the egg mixture covers the base evenly.

6 **B** Count to ten, then use a wooden spoon to pull the set egg from the sides of the pan, towards the middle. Doing this allows the runny egg to move to the edge of the pan, so that the omelette cooks evenly. This will take about a minute.

7 When the bottom is cooked but there is still some runny egg on top, sprinkle over the grated cheese.

8 Slide the palette knife under one side of the omelette and quickly fold it over. Quickly tilt the pan so the omelette slides, still folded, on to your plate.

batter

The batters for toad in the hole, Yorkshire puddings, pancakes and drop scones are all made in a similar way, but the quantities of ingredients may vary.

toad in the hole

SERVES 4

Don't open the oven while these toads are cooking, because the cold air will make the batter collapse.

YOU WILL NEED:

INGREDIENTS
- 125g (4½oz) plain flour
- a pinch of sea salt and freshly ground black pepper
- 125ml (4½fl oz) milk
- 125ml (4½fl oz) water
- 2 large eggs
- 6 tsp vegetable oil
- 12 tiny good-quality chipolata or cocktail sausages

EQUIPMENT
- sieve
- large bowl
- 2 jugs
- small bowl
- fork
- wooden spoon
- whisk
- 12-hole muffin tin
- oven gloves
- kitchen tongs
- palette knife

1 Turn the oven on to 220°C/ 425°F/gas mark 7.

2 To make the batter (see page 62), sieve the flour into a large bowl, then add the salt and pepper. Make a well in the middle of the flour.

3 Mix the milk and water together in a jug. Crack the eggs into a small bowl and beat together lightly with a fork.

4 Pour the eggs into the well in the flour. Use a wooden spoon to gradually stir the eggs into the flour. As the mixture thickens, pour in the milk and water a little at a time and whisk until you have a smooth batter. Pour the batter into a clean jug.

5 Put ½ teaspoon of oil into each hole in a muffin tin. Using oven gloves, put the tin into the oven for 5 minutes. Using oven gloves, take the tin out of the oven and put on to a pan stand – the oil will be really hot so be careful; you may need to get an adult to help.

6 Using kitchen tongs, put a chipolata into each hole in the tin. Using oven gloves, put the tin back into the oven for 15 minutes, until the sausages are golden brown. Using oven gloves, take the tin out of the oven and rest on a pan stand. Pour the batter into the muffin holes.

7 Using oven gloves, put the tin straight into the oven for 12–14 minutes, until the batter has puffed up and is golden brown and crispy.

8 Using oven gloves, remove the tin from the oven. Leave to cool in the tin for 1 minute before using a palette knife to remove each toad from the tin. Serve straight away.

batter

blueberry pancakes

SERVES 4

Blueberry pancakes are usually eaten for breakfast in America, often drizzled with warm maple syrup.

YOU WILL NEED:

INGREDIENTS

- 125g (4½oz) apples
- 15g (½oz) unsalted butter, plus a little knob for frying
- 1 large egg
- 280ml (9½fl oz) buttermilk
- 2 drops of vanilla extract
- 125g (4½oz) plain flour
- 1 tsp bicarbonate of soda
- ½ tsp ground cinnamon
- 125g (4½oz) fresh blueberries
- 1 tsp vegetable oil
- 4 tbsp maple or golden syrup or honey, to serve

EQUIPMENT

- vegetable peeler
- knife
- 2 small saucepans
- 2 large bowls
- whisk
- sieve
- wooden spoon
- frying pan
- spoon
- palette knife
- plate
- kitchen foil
- small jug

1 Peel, core and chop the apples into pieces the same size as the blueberries.

2 Put the 15g (½oz) butter into a small saucepan and melt over a medium heat. Remove from the heat and allow to cool slightly.

3 Put the egg, buttermilk, vanilla and melted butter into a large bowl and whisk. Sieve the flour, bicarbonate of soda and cinnamon into another large bowl and make a well in the centre.

4 Pour the egg mixture into the well and use a wooden spoon to stir the liquid to make a whirlpool in the middle of the bowl. This will gradually pull the flour into the liquid – don't stir the flour, just keep stirring the liquid. Don't over-mix the batter; lumps are fine. When it is well combined, stir in the apples and blueberries.

5 Heat the oil and knob of butter in a frying pan until the butter just starts to bubble.

6 Drop spoonfuls of batter into the pan, spaced well apart so they don't stick together. Cook for 2 minutes, until bubbles start to rise on the surface. Slide a palette knife under each pancake and quickly flip it over.

7 Cook for another 2 minutes, then lift the pancakes out on to a plate using the palette knife. Cover the plate with foil to keep the pancakes warm. Cook the remaining batter in the same way.

8 Put the maple or golden syrup or honey into a small saucepan and warm very gently over a medium heat. Pour the syrup into a jug and serve it drizzled over the warm pancakes.

batter

pancakes

MAKES 12 PANCAKES

These pancakes taste delicious with fresh fruit, lemon and sugar, or even jam.

YOU WILL NEED:

INGREDIENTS
- 115g (4oz) plain flour
- a pinch of salt
- 2 large eggs
- 200ml (7fl oz) milk
- 100ml (3½fl oz) water
- 30g (1oz) butter, melted, plus a little extra for frying
- 1 tbsp vegetable oil

EQUIPMENT
- sieve and small jug
- 1 large and 1 small bowl
- fork
- small wooden spoon and hand whisk
- spatula and tea-towel
- frying pan, palette knife and plate
- kitchen foil

GOOD THINGS TO EAT WITH PANCAKES
- ✔ freshly squeezed lemon juice and caster sugar
- ✔ strawberry jam
- ✔ sliced bananas and soft brown sugar
- ✔ chocolate spread

1 Sieve the flour and salt into a large bowl, holding the sieve high above the bowl. Tap an egg firmly against the side of a small bowl, push your thumbs into the crack, and carefully pull the shell apart, letting the egg drop into the bowl. Repeat with the second egg. Beat the eggs with a fork until the whites and yolks are mixed.

2 Mix the milk and water together in a small jug. Make a well in the centre of the flour. Pour in the beaten eggs and 2 tablespoons of the milk mixture. **(A)** Using a small wooden spoon, stir the eggs and milk to make a whirlpool in the middle of the bowl. This will gradually pull the flour into the liquid. Don't stir in the flour – just keep stirring the liquid. When the liquid is as thick as double cream, pour in a little more milk mixture and continue to mix, pulling in more flour.

3 Continue, alternately mixing and adding liquid, until all the milk is used up. Run a spatula around the bowl to dislodge any bits of flour and beat the mixture so you have a smooth, lump-free batter. **(B)** Using a whisk, beat in the melted butter. Leave the batter to stand, covered with a tea-towel, for at least 30 minutes.

4 Put 1 teaspoon of oil and a little butter in a frying pan over a medium heat. When hot, pour 3 tablespoons of batter into the pan. Swirl the mixture around the pan so that the base is covered, then pour any excess mixture back into the bowl.

5 Cook the pancake for a minute or so, then use a palette knife to flip it over. Cook for another minute or so, then tip it out on to a plate. Cover with foil to keep warm. Keep making pancakes until all the batter is used up – you may need to add more oil and butter to the pan after 6 pancakes.

whisking

You whisk things to add air to them, which makes dishes lighter and fluffier. There are a few types of whisks: a big food mixer with a whisk attachment, a hand-held electric whisk, or a simple hand whisk. All of these work fine, but some are quicker than others. Many dishes, such as meringue or chocolate mousse, look and taste fantastic because some of the ingredients are whisked. As well as making a dish lighter, air bubbles act as a raising agent – they heat up in the oven and get bigger, making dishes, such as cakes or soufflés, even lighter. Stiff peaks occur when the egg foam holds its shape firmly and no longer wobbles on the tip of the whisk. Ideally the foam should not be too dry; it should still look slightly moist. Try not to over-whisk the foam because it can then collapse.

YOU WILL NEED:

INGREDIENTS
- eggs

EQUIPMENT
- 1 large bowl and 2 small bowls
- teaspoon and tea-towel
- hand whisk (optional) and electric whisk

WHAT TO USE WHISKING FOR
✔ fruit fools
✔ mousses
✔ soufflés
✔ whisked cakes
✔ soufflé omelettes that puff up in the pan

1 **A** Tap your first egg firmly against the side of a large, clean, dry bowl, push your thumbs into the crack, and carefully pull the shell apart, keeping the yolk in one half of the shell. Tip the yolk from one half of the shell to the other, letting the white dribble into the bowl. Put the yolk in a small bowl.

2 Break the second egg over a second small bowl. Tip the white into the big bowl and put the yolks together. Continue like this until you have as many egg whites as you need.

3 Check the whites for any bits of yolk or shell and remove with a teaspoon or empty shell half.

4 Rest the bowl of egg whites on a tea-towel so it doesn't slip around. **B** The first time you use a whisk, use a hand whisk to get a feel for whisking, but then swap to an electric whisk. Put the whisk in the bowl and begin at a low speed. Gradually increase the speed, moving the whisk in a figure-of-eight movement until the whites increase in volume and turn from clear to white.

5 Keep whisking until stiff peaks form: if you tip the bowl gently the peaks of the whites should slightly tip over. The egg whites are now ready to have sugar whisked in or to be folded into another mixture as they are into an omelette or soufflé.

whisking

toffee meringues with honeycomb cream

MAKES APPROX 30 LARGE OR 40 TINY MERINGUES

Who'd believe that something so yummy could be made out of egg whites? In the summer, when soft fruit is in season, such as raspberries and strawberries, try adding a handful to some whipped cream and use to sandwich your meringues together.

YOU WILL NEED:

INGREDIENTS
- 3 medium egg whites
- 100g (3½oz) golden caster sugar
- 75g (2¾oz) light soft brown sugar
- 250ml (9fl oz) double cream
- 2 Crunchie bars (honeycomb coated in chocolate) or home-made honeycomb (see page 174)

EQUIPMENT
- 2 baking sheets
- baking parchment
- 3 large bowls
- electric whisk
- tablespoon
- oven gloves
- plate
- plastic sandwich bag
- rolling pin
- metal spoon

1 Turn the oven on to 110°C/225°F/gas mark ¼. Line 2 baking sheets with baking parchment.

2 Separate the eggs (see page 63, point 1). Put the egg whites into a large bowl and whisk until stiff peaks form (see page 63, points 4 and 5).

3 In a second large bowl, combine the two sugars. Whisk 1 tablespoon of sugar into the egg whites. Add more sugar a spoonful at a time, whisking well after each spoonful, until half of the sugar is used up. Whisk in the remaining half in one go, until the mixture is thick and glossy.

4 Dot a little meringue mixture under the corners of the baking paper to help stick it to the trays. Use a tablespoon to put blobs of the mixture on the lined trays, leaving space between them. Wearing oven gloves, put the baking sheets in the oven. Cook for 1 hour.

5 Use oven gloves to take the meringues out of the oven. The middle of the meringues will be slightly squidgy. When the meringues are cool, gently lift them off the paper and rest on a plate.

6 Put the cream in a clean large bowl and whisk it until soft peaks form. Put the honeycomb into a plastic bag and bash it with a rolling pin to make small pieces. Add the broken honeycomb to the whipped cream and, using a metal spoon, mix gently.

7 Spoon 1 tablespoon of the honeycomb mixture on to the flat side of one of the meringues and sandwich another meringue on top. Repeat with the rest of the meringues and cream.

shortcrust pastry

MAKES ENOUGH TO LINE A 23CM (9 INCH) TART TIN

Once you have learnt how to make pastry you can make lots of new things but jam tarts (see opposite) are about the easiest!

YOU WILL NEED:

INGREDIENTS
- 225g (8oz) plain flour, plus extra for dusting
- pinch of salt
- 115g (4oz) cold butter
- 1–2 tbsp very cold water

EQUIPMENT
- sieve
- large bowl
- table knife
- tablespoon
- clingfilm
- rolling pin

1 Sieve the flour and salt into a large mixing bowl, holding the sieve high above the bowl so the flour gets a good airing

2 Cut the cold butter into small pieces then stir it into the flour using a knife. Rub the butter into the flour by dipping your fingertips into the flour and gently rub the little pieces of butter between the tips of your thumbs and fingers so that they flatten and gradually mix into the flour. As you do this keep lifting your hands up above the rim of the bowl as this will let air get into the flour and keep the mixture cool.

3 Gently shake the bowl occasionally as this will make bits of butter come to the surface and you can rub them in. Keep rubbing in as lightly as you can until you cannot see any more bits of butter and the mixture looks like coarse breadcrumbs. Try to do the rubbing in as quickly as possible because the longer you touch the butter the hotter it will become and your mixture may become greasy and sticky. If this happens just put the bowl in the refrigerator for 5 minutes and then continue.

4 Wash your hands, then run them under cold water and dry them thoroughly. (A) Sprinkle 1 tablespoon of cold water over the mixture and quickly mix it in with the knife. The pastry will start to come together in small lumps. If there are any dry bits of flour in the bottom of the bowl sprinkle over a tiny bit more water and mix again. It is very important not to add too much liquid as the pastry will become sticky and difficult to roll out, and when it is cooked the pastry will be tough and hard.

5 (B) Use your hands to bring the pastry together in a ball. This is easiest if you use a wiping motion and wipe all the little bits up into one big ball. The dough should feel like plasticine – not too hard and not too soft. Tip it out on to a floured work-surface and knead it for a second or two just to bring it into a smooth ball. Wrap the pastry in a piece of clingfilm and leave to rest in the refrigerator for 30 minutes,

6 Clear down the work-surface, make sure it is really dry and sprinkle it with a little flour.

7 Take the pastry out of the refrigerator, unwrap it from the clingfilm and set it on the floured work surface. Flour your hands and a rolling pin.

8 Pat the dough down a little so the surface is flat. Use the rolling pin to roll the pastry away from you in gentle strokes, pressing down with it gently as you go. After every two or three strokes give the pastry a quarter turn – this will ensure you have a round of pastry rather than a long thin strip. Keep rolling until the pastry is the required thickness – generally the smaller the tin you are lining, the thinner the pastry should be.

sweet shortcrust pastry

Once you have mastered making a plain shortcrust pastry for savoury dishes, such as tarts and quiches, you could have a go at making sweet pastry. There are many variations, but one of the simplest is to add a little sugar for sweetness and an egg yolk for a rich flavour and texture. You can also change the flavour of the pastry by adding a little cocoa powder to the mixture (see page 146).

fruity jam tarts

MAKES 18

Try using different kinds of jam when you make these so you have a plateful of lovely jewel-like tarts.

YOU WILL NEED:

INGREDIENTS
- 225g (8oz) plain flour, plus extra for dusting
- 115g (4oz) chilled butter, cut into small pieces, plus a little extra for greasing
- 1 tsp golden caster sugar
- 1 large egg yolk
- 1–2 tbsp cold water
- 18 heaped tsp jam, such as raspberry, apricot, strawberry or blackcurrant

EQUIPMENT
- sieve
- large bowl
- table knife
- clingfilm
- rolling pin
- fluted biscuit cutter approx 7.5cm (3 inch) diameter
- 2 x12-hole jam tart tins
- fork
- oven gloves
- teaspoon
- palette knife
- wire rack

1 Sieve the flour into a large bowl, then add the butter and rub it in using your fingertips until the mixture looks like coarse breadcrumbs.

2 Add the sugar and mix together. Use a knife to mix in the egg yolk, then add the water, a little at a time, stirring with the knife until the mixture comes together and you can form a ball with your hands. See opposite for a step-by-step guide to making pastry.

3 Wrap the pastry in a piece of clingfilm and put it in the refrigerator for 30 minutes – this will make it easier to roll out.

4 Turn the oven on to 200°C/400°F/gas mark 6. Rub the tart tins with a little butter. Take the pastry out of the refrigerator and unwrap it. Ⓐ Sprinkle your work-surface and your rolling pin with a little flour and roll the pastry out to about 3–4mm (⅛ inch) thick.

5 Dip the cutter in flour, then cut circles – you may need to gather the bits of pastry up and roll them out again to make 18. Lay the rounds in the tart tin and press them into place. Prick the base of each tart once with a fork.

6 Use oven gloves to put the tart tray in the oven. Bake for 6 minutes, until the pastry is pale golden. Using oven gloves, take the tray out of the oven. Ⓑ Put 1 teaspoon of jam into each tart and, using oven gloves, put the tray back into the oven for 6 minutes. Using oven gloves, take the tray out and leave the tarts to cool for a few minutes, then use a palette knife to gently lift them out of the tin to cool completely on a wire rack.

sweet shortcrust pastry

white choc and raspberry tarts

MAKES 12

A great idea for an easy, but impressive, pudding that is really good fun to make.

YOU WILL NEED:
INGREDIENTS
- 175g (6oz) plain flour, plus extra for dusting
- 3 tsp good-quality cocoa powder
- 1 heaped tbsp icing sugar
- 75g (2¾oz) cold butter, cut into small cubes
- 1 large egg yolk
- 1 tsp cold water
- a little icing sugar, for dusting

for the filling:
- 100g (3½oz) good-quality white chocolate
- 100ml (3½fl oz) double cream
- 250g (9oz) raspberries

EQUIPMENT
- sieve
- large bowl
- knife
- clingfilm
- rolling pin
- cutter 10cm (4 inch) diameter
- 12-hole tart tin
- fork
- oven gloves
- medium bowl
- medium saucepan
- small wooden spoon
- small palette knife
- spoon

1 Sieve the flour, cocoa and icing sugar into a large bowl. Rub in the cold butter. Stir in the egg yolk and water until the pastry starts to come together, then use your hands to bring everything together in a ball (see page 145, points 1–2).

2 Tip it out on to a floured work-surface and knead it for a second or 2 just to bring it together in a smooth ball, then wrap it in clingfilm and leave it to rest in the refrigerator for 30 minutes.

3 Turn the oven on to 200°C/400°F/gas mark 6. Rub the tart tin with a little butter. Take the pastry out of the refrigerator and unwrap it. Sprinkle your work surface and rolling pin with a little flour and roll the pastry out to about 3–4mm (⅛ inch) thick.

4 Cut out as many circles as you can – you may need to gather the bits of pastry up and roll them out again to make 12 circles. Lay the rounds of pastry in the tart tin and press them gently into place. Prick the bases of the tarts with a fork and, using oven gloves, put them into the oven for 6–8 minutes.

5 Using oven gloves, take the tin out of the oven and leave to cool.

6 Break the chocolate up into small pieces and put into a medium bowl over a pan of gently simmering water. When the chocolate has melted, leave it to cool slightly – if you dip a clean finger into it should feel the same temperature as your finger.

7 Pour the cream into the chocolate and stir until it is just mixed together.

8 Use a small palette knife to lift the tart cases out of the tin and carefully fill each one with a generous spoonful of the cream mixture. Top each one with a few fresh raspberries, dust with a little icing sugar and serve straight away.

cookies

A cookie is a small, crisp pastry, either sweet or savoury, or a soft and/or chewy small cake. There are many ways to make cookies, but this recipe uses the 'creaming method' of beating butter and sugar together until light to incorporate air. Eggs are then added before the flour, cocoa and chocolate.

American chocolate orange cookies

MAKES 18 COOKIES

YOU WILL NEED:
INGREDIENTS
- 100g (3½oz) each of orange-flavoured milk chocolate and white chocolate
- 100g (3½oz) butter, softened
- 100g (3½oz) light soft brown sugar
- 2 drops of vanilla extract
- 1 medium egg
- 2 tbsp golden syrup
- 150g (5½oz) self-raising flour
- 2 tbsp good-quality cocoa powder

EQUIPMENT
- baking sheets and baking parchment
- chopping board and knife
- large bowl, wooden spoon and sieve
- oven gloves

OTHER GOOD THINGS TO ADD TO COOKIES
✔ toasted chopped nuts, e.g. hazelnuts, pecans or walnuts
✔ dried fruit, e.g. raisins, sultanas
✔ different type of chocolate chunks, e.g. milk, white or dark

1   Turn the oven on to 180°C/350°F/gas mark 4. Line 2 baking sheets with baking parchment.

2   Put the chocolate on to a chopping board and chop it into big chunks using a knife.

3   (A) Put the butter, sugar and vanilla into a large bowl and beat together using a wooden spoon until the mixture is pale and fluffy.

4   Add the egg and golden syrup and beat for 2 more minutes.

5   Sieve the flour and cocoa powder into the bowl and gently mix it in until the mixture is smooth. (B) Stir in the chocolate chunks.

6   Spoon walnut-sized blobs of the mixture on to the prepared baking sheets, allowing space for them to spread.

7   Use your oven gloves to put the trays into the oven and cook for 7 minutes. Remove the trays from the oven with your oven gloves and leave to cool until the cookies are firm, then carefully peel them off the baking paper.

8   Eat straight away or store in an airtight tin.

krispies

Although this isn't strictly a technique, it seemed to be impossible to write a cookery book for children without including this all-time favourite. If you make these at Easter time, make them into nests. When you have put the mixture into the cases, use a metal teaspoon to make a hollow in the middle of each krispie, like a nest. When they have set you can rest some chocolate eggs in the hollow.

toffee marshmallow krispies

MAKES 12

YOU WILL NEED:

INGREDIENTS
- 75g (2¾oz) toffees, unwrapped
- 75g (2¾oz) unsalted butter
- 75g (2¾oz) marshmallows
- 1 tbsp golden syrup
- 75g (2¾oz) rice krispies

EQUIPMENT
- 12 paper cases
- 12-hole muffin tray
- large saucepan
- wooden spoon
- spatula
- metal spoon

1 Put the paper cases into the holes of the muffin tray.

2 Put the toffees, butter, marshmallows and golden syrup into a saucepan.

3 (A) Heat very gently, stirring occasionally with a wooden spoon, until everything is melted and the mixture is smooth – this will take about 3 minutes.

4 (B) Take the pan off the heat and add the rice krispies. Stir everything together – this is easiest using a plastic spatula so you can scrape up all the sticky liquid from the bottom of the pan.

5 Working quickly, before the mixture sets, use a metal spoon to put spoonfuls of the mixture into the paper cases until all the mixture is used up.

6 Leave the krispies to set for at least an hour. Eat straight away or store in an airtight container.

flapjacks

A flapjack should not be too sweet or sticky and similarly not too 'oaty'.

classic tea-time flapjacks

MAKES 15

YOU WILL NEED:
INGREDIENTS
- butter, for greasing
- 80g (2¾oz) light soft brown sugar
- 180g (6½oz) butter
- 150g (5½oz) golden syrup
- 335g (11¾oz) oats

EQUIPMENT
- 25cm (10 inch) tin with 2.5cm (1 inch) high sides
- large saucepan and wooden spoon
- oven gloves, knife and wire rack

OTHER GOOD THINGS TO ADD TO FLAPJACKS
✔ chopped dried fruit, such as apricots or sultanas
✔ chopped toasted nuts, such as hazelnuts or pecan nuts
✔ seeds, such as sesame seeds, pumpkin seeds
✔ they are also good half dipped in melted chocolate – just dip them and leave them to cool on some baking parchment

1 Turn the oven on to 180°C/350°F/gas mark 4.

2 Rub the butter lightly over the base and sides of the tin.

3 Put the sugar, butter and golden syrup into a pan. Heat gently over a low heat until the butter is melted and the sugar has dissolved, stirring often with a wooden spoon. Turn the heat up and bring the mixture to the boil. Turn the heat off immediately.

4 (A) Put the oats into the pan. Stir with the wooden spoon until there are no pockets of dry oats – they should be covered in the syrup mixture.

5 (B) Tip the mixture into the prepared tin and spread it out evenly right to the edges. Use the back of the spoon to smooth the top.

6 Using oven gloves, put the tin into the oven and bake for 10-15 minutes until golden.

7 Using oven gloves, take the tray out of the oven and leave the flapjacks to cool for 5 minutes.

8 While the flapjacks are still warm, use a knife to mark them into squares. Leave to cool completely then lift them out on to a wire rack. Eat straight awat or store in an airtight container.

popcorn

Popcorn is very easy to cook, but as you need to get the oil quite hot you should ask an adult to help you. A lot of people wonder how corn pops. Well, inside each hard little corn there is some water – not much, but enough. When the corn is heated, the water turns to steam, which is a gas that needs more space than water. The only way for it to find space is to break out of the corn by exploding, making the corn kernels pop open.

sweet popcorn

MAKES A BIG BOWLFUL

YOU WILL NEED:

INGREDIENTS
- 2 tbsp sunflower oil
- 65g (2½oz) popping corn
- 2 tsp golden caster sugar (optional)

EQUIPMENT
- large heavy-based saucepan with lid
- wooden spoon and serving bowl

OTHER GOOD THINGS TO ADD TO POPCORN
- ✔ vanilla sugar instead of ordinary sugar
- ✔ soft light brown sugar for a more toffee-ish flavour
- ✔ 1 tbsp of golden syrup or maple syrup
- ✔ mix a pinch of ground cinnamon into your sugar
- ✔ for savoury popcorn, try adding crunchy peanut butter (about 2 tbsp), or 50g (1¾oz) finely grated Cheddar or Parmesan

1 Put the oil into a large saucepan and heat until the oil is hot. Tip the corn into the pan, spreading it out so it covers the base of the pan.

2 Cook the corn until it starts to pop, then put on the lid straight away. (If you have a pan with a glass lid this is fun to watch.)

3 Cook the corn for 2–3 more minutes. Hold the lid on tightly and shake the pan often. Keep cooking until the sound of popping corn stops.

4 Remove from the heat, take off the lid and pour over the sugar. Stir gently with a wooden spoon and tip into a serving bowl. Eat straight away.

6 FROM AFAR

stir-frying vegetables

Stir-frying is a quick method of cooking used mainly for Chinese food. You will need to use a wok or a very large frying pan and you must cook the food quickly over a very high heat. To make sure the food is cooked evenly you will need to keep stirring the ingredients around in the pan, which is why it is called 'stir-frying'.

Chinese stir-fry with cashew nuts

SERVES 4

YOU WILL NEED:

INGREDIENTS

- 1 red pepper
- 2.5cm (1 inch) piece of fresh root ginger
- 3 spring onions, trimmed
- 1 garlic clove, peeled and crushed
- 1 small ripe pineapple
- 200g (7oz) mangetout or sugar snap peas
- 2 tbsp vegetable oil
- 3 tsp sesame oil
- 200g (7oz) bean sprouts
- 50g (1¾oz) cashew nuts
- 1 tbsp light soy sauce
- freshly ground black pepper
- 200g (7oz) egg thread noodles, boiled according to the packet instructions

EQUIPMENT

- garlic crusher
- large saucepan
- colander
- chopping board
- knife
- vegetable peeler
- small bowl
- large plate
- wok or frying pan
- wooden spatula

1 Using a chopping board and a knife, cut the red pepper in half, remove the seeds and thinly slice the flesh.

2 Peel the ginger and finely chop it. Thinly slice the spring onions. Place in a small bowl with the garlic. Put the pineapple on to a board, cut off its bottom and crown (the top part where the leaves stick out), then lay it flat-side down and cut the skin off the flesh – see page 118. Pick out the eyes (the little round brown circles) and cut the flesh into bite-sized pieces. Keep all the vegetables, including the peas, and pineapple in separate bundles on a plate.

3 Heat a wok or frying pan over a high heat until very hot. Pour in the oils (see page 160, point 3). **A** Add the garlic, ginger and spring onions and stir around with a wooden spatula for 1 minute.

4 **B** Cook the hardest vegetables first, so start by adding the pepper and mangetout or sugar snap peas and cook for 1 minute. Add the pineapple chunks, bean sprouts and cashew nuts and keep stirring for 1 minute.

5 Add the soy sauce and season with freshly ground black pepper. As soon as the vegetables are cooked, but still crunchy, add the noodles. Mix everything together and eat straight away.

stir-frying vegetables

Stir-frying is a fast method of cooking that can be used to fry meat, fish or vegetables. The following guidelines will help to make sure that you find it both easy and successful.

to stir-fry:

1   Prepare all your ingredients before you begin cooking. All the chopping, slicing and getting sauces ready has to be done before you start to stir-fry. Have everything laid out ready to go, a bit like how you often see it on TV. This is really important to make sure that you do not overcook or undercook any of the ingredients.

2   If you are using noodles or rice make sure that they have been soaked and drained, or cooked, before you begin stir-frying.

3   Put the wok (or frying pan) over the heat and heat until really hot before you add the oil. Once you add the oil, swirl it around the pan and then add your other ingredients straight away.

4   You will need to adjust the heat as you stir-fry – turning it up when you add more food to the wok and down a little when the food starts to cook.

5   When you become more confident with a wok and stir-frying, you can move the food that is cooked to the top part of the wok – furthest away from the heat – while the remaining ingredients cook at the bottom.

6   The first ingredients to go in the wok should be those that will take the longest to cook. For example, carrots and broccoli will take longer to cook than spring onions or bean sprouts. This is worth thinking about if you are adding your own vegetables and not following a recipe.

7   Try experimenting with different ingredients in your stir-fries: fruit, such as pineapple, and nuts, such as cashew nuts (see page 159), can add lots of flavour and texture to your finished meal.

curry paste

A curry paste is an intensely flavoured mixture of herbs and spices that is used in curries and other dishes. This is a Thai red curry paste. Store in an airtight container in the refrigerator – a jam jar is ideal. Be careful when chopping chillies: wash your hands thoroughly afterwards and don't touch your face, especially your eyes – the chilli juice can really sting!

curry paste

MAKES APPROX 4 TABLESPOONS

YOU WILL NEED:

INGREDIENTS
- 6 medium red chillies
- 2 sticks of lemon grass
- 2.5cm (1 inch) piece of fresh root ginger
- 2 shallots
- 3 garlic cloves
- 1 tsp each of coriander seeds, cumin seeds and black peppercorns
- 1 tsp lime zest
- 1 tbsp lime juice
- 2 tbsp fresh coriander

EQUIPMENT
- lemon zester
- chopping board
- knife
- tall jug
- vegetable peeler
- frying pan
- hand-held blender or small food processor

1 Use a chopping board and a knife to prepare the ingredients.

2 Cut the chillies in half, scoop out the seeds and finely chop. Put into a tall jug.

3 Remove the tough outer layer of the lemon grass stalks and finely chop what's left, but throw away the tough ends. Add to the chillies.

4 **A** Peel the fresh root ginger and finely chop the flesh, then add to the chillies and lemon grass.

5 Peel the shallots and finely chop, and add to the other ingredients.

6 Peel the garlic and finely chop, adding to the rest.

7 **B** Put the coriander seeds, cumin seeds and black peppercorns into a dry frying pan. Heat over a high heat until the seeds just start to pop. This dry-frying helps to bring out the flavour of the spices.

8 Add the aromatics, lime zest and juice along with the fresh coriander to the jug and use a hand-held blender to blitz the mixture to a paste. Alternatively, put all the prepared ingredients into a small food processor and blitz to make a paste in the same way.

curry paste

Amanda's Thai red fish curry

SERVES 4–5

Many of the ingredients for a Thai curry, such as kaffir lime leaves and red curry paste, can be found in supermarkets now, but you'll also find good quality ingredients in many delis and Chinese/Thai supermarkets. If you can't find kaffir lime leaves you could use some lime zest instead. Special thanks to Amanda, a wonderful friend, for sharing her curry secrets, on which this recipe is based.

YOU WILL NEED:

INGREDIENTS
- 500g (1lb 2oz) salmon fillet, monkfish, etc
- 600g (1lb 5oz) squash (you will need 400g/14oz peeled weight)
- 3 pak choi
- 1 tbsp groundnut oil
- 1-2 tbsp good-quality Thai red curry paste (see page 161)
- ½ tsp turmeric
- 400ml (14fl oz) coconut milk
- 350ml (12fl oz) fish stock
- 3 tbsp fish sauce, plus extra to taste
- 2 tsp golden caster sugar
- 3–5 lemon grass stalks, bruised (bashed with a rolling pin to split them open slightly)
- 6 kaffir lime leaves
- half a bunch fresh coriander, chopped
- freshly ground black pepper
- steamed Thai jasmine rice, to serve

EQUIPMENT
- vegetable peeler
- rolling pin
- saucepan and lid
- tweezers
- chopping board
- knife
- bowl
- metal spoon
- large heavy-based saucepan
- wooden spoon
- ladle

1 Run your fingers over the fish to check for bones. If you find any, pick them out with your fingers or use a pair of tweezers.

2 Using a chopping board and a knife, cut the fish into large bite-sized pieces and put in a bowl.

3 Cut the squash in half, scoop out the seeds using a metal spoon, and then cut the flesh into bite-sized pieces. Cut the pak choi into same-size pieces.

4 Heat the oil in a large saucepan and add the curry paste. It will start to sizzle – cook for about 2 minutes, stirring continuously with a wooden spoon. Add the turmeric and stir for a few seconds.

5 Pour in the coconut milk, fish stock and fish sauce and add the caster sugar, lemon grass and lime leaves. Stir well and then bring up to a gentle simmer.

6 Add the squash and cook for 12 minutes or until just cooked – you should be able to easily poke the squash with a knife.

7 Now add the fish, pak choi and half the fresh coriander and cook for 5 minutes, or until the fish is cooked.

8 Add more fish sauce and freshly ground black pepper to taste. Sprinkle over the remaining coriander. Ladle the steamed rice into bowls and then top with the curry.

marinades

Fish, meat and vegetables (see page 31) can all be marinated before being cooked. Marinades not only add flavour to the food, but can also help to tenderize meat before cooking. These are a few marinade ideas for lamb, chicken and fish. Once you have all the ingredients together in a large bowl, mix well and gently massage the marinade into the meat or fish with your fingers. Cover with clingfilm and place in the refrigerator until you're ready to cook. The longer you leave the meat, the deeper the flavour it will have of the marinade. Overnight is often ideal, but a few hours will do – although if you are going to marinate fish in lemon juice, only leave the fish in the juice for 10 minutes or so as the juice will start to cook the fish. If you find the garlic too overpowering for the fish, simply remove the crushed cloves before you start to cook it.

You can use a pastry brush to brush any remaining marinade on to the meat and fish while cooking.

for approx 500g (1lb 2oz) cubed lamb or chicken

- juice of 1 lemon
- 5 tbsp olive oil
- 1 tbsp chopped fresh oregano
- 1 small onion, sliced
- 1–2 garlic cloves, peeled and crushed

Thread the marinated cubes of lamb or chicken on to metal or pre-soaked wooden skewers (see page 31). Place on the grill of a hot barbecue or underneath a hot grill and turn occasionally until cooked through (see page 30, point 7). This should take around 20-25 minutes.

for 6 chicken drumsticks

- 2 tbsp runny honey
- 1 tbsp soy sauce
- 5mm (⅕ inch) piece of fresh root ginger. peeled and chopped
- 100ml (3½ fl oz) yoghurt
- juice of ½ lemon
- 2 garlic cloves, peeled and chopped
- large pinch of paprika

Using oven gloves, place the marinated drumsticks in a roasting tin in an oven preheated to 200°C/400°F/gas mark 6 and cook for 30 minutes, or until cooked through (see page 44, point 4).

for 500g (1lb 2oz) fresh cubed fish such as monkfish

- handful of fresh chopped herbs
- 2 tbsp olive oil
- juice of 1 lemon
- 5cm (2 inch) piece of fresh root ginger, peeled and chopped
- 1 tbsp soy sauce
- 2 tsp sesame oil
- 1–2 garlic cloves, peeled and crushed
- 2 spring onions, chopped

Thread the marinated cubes of monkfish on to metal or pre-soaked wooden skewers (see page 31). Place on the grill of a hot barbecue or underneath a hot grill and turn occasionally until just cooked (see page 12, point 5). This shouldn't take longer than a few minutes.

marinades

sticky spare ribs

SERVES 4

These are good fun to make and even more fun to eat!

YOU WILL NEED:

INGREDIENTS

- 1 garlic clove, peeled
- 2 tbsp tomato purée
- 2 tbsp dark muscovado sugar
- 2 tbsp light soy sauce
- 1 tbsp red wine vinegar
- 1 tbsp honey
- 1 tbsp vegetable oil
- 250ml (9fl oz) orange juice
- salt and freshly ground black pepper
- 20 uncooked pork spare ribs – approx 950g (2lb 2oz)

EQUIPMENT

- knife
- garlic crusher
- medium bowl
- small whisk
- large roasting tin
- oven gloves
- wooden spoon

1 Turn the oven on to 180°C/350°F/gas mark 4.

2 Crush the garlic in a garlic crusher and put into a bowl. Add the tomato purée, sugar, soy sauce, vinegar, honey, oil and orange juice. Season with pepper and a pinch of salt, then whisk until it is smooth.

3 Lay the ribs in a roasting tin in a single layer. Pour over half the sauce. Turn the ribs to make sure they are completely covered.

4 Using oven gloves, put the ribs in the oven and cook for 20 minutes, then take them out and give them a really good stir and put back in the oven for another 10 minutes. Use oven gloves to take them out of the oven again and pour over the remaining marinade. Give them another really good stir and put them back in the oven for a further 15–20 minutes.

5 Using oven gloves, remove the roasting tin from the oven. These are delicious served with rice and salad.

marinades

pesto-marinated chicken drumsticks

SERVES 3

A few simple ingredients make a wonderful marinade. You can buy ready-made pesto from supermarkets and delis.

YOU WILL NEED:

INGREDIENTS
- 1 garlic clove, peeled
- 2 tbsp pesto
- 2 tbsp olive oil
- 2 tbsp lemon juice
- salt and freshly ground black pepper
- 6 chicken drumsticks (approx 750g/ 1lb 10oz)

EQUIPMENT
- garlic crusher
- large bowl
- spoon
- knife
- chopping board
- clingfilm
- roasting tin
- oven gloves
- kitchen tongs

1 Using a garlic crusher, crush the garlic and put into a large bowl. Add the pesto, oil and lemon juice. Season with salt and freshly ground black pepper. Mix together with a spoon.

2 Using a knife and a chopping board, carefully cut small slits into the chicken drumsticks without cutting all the way through to the bone.

3 Add the chicken drumsticks to the pesto mixture.

4 Using your clean hands, really massage the marinade into the chicken, making sure it coats the chicken thoroughly. Wash your hands. Cover the bowl with clingfilm and leave the chicken to marinate in the refrigerator for at least half an hour or longer if possible.

5 Turn the oven to 200°C/400°F/gas mark 6. Spoon the chicken and any juices into a roasting tin and, using oven gloves, put into the oven. Cook for 30 minutes or until cooked through (see page 44, point 4).

6 Lift the drumsticks out of the tin with tongs, leaving the fat in the tin.

using cutters

You can use pretty shaped cutters, such as hearts or flowers, to cut out biscuits. They're great for themed parties, such as Christmas or Halloween.

Billy's rhubarb and custard biscuits

MAKES 18–20

Try adding a little cocoa to the mixture instead of custard powder for chocolate biscuits.

YOU WILL NEED:

INGREDIENTS
- 85g (3oz) butter
- 85g (3oz) golden caster sugar
- 115g (4oz) plain flour, plus extra for rolling out
- 3 tbsp instant custard powder (the kind that you add milk, not water, to)
- 18–20 rhubarb and custard flavoured boiled sweets

EQUIPMENT
- 2 baking sheets
- baking parchment
- large bowl
- wooden spoon
- sieve
- knife
- rolling pin
- 5cm (2 inch) and 1.5cm (⅝ inch) cutters
- palette knife
- oven gloves
- wire rack
- large white plate

1 Turn the oven to 180°C/350°F/gas mark 4. Line 2 baking sheets with parchment.

2 Put the butter and sugar together in a large bowl and, using a wooden spoon, beat together until pale and creamy.

3 Sieve the flour and custard powder into the butter and sugar mixture and stir to mix well, until it comes together to form a dough.

4 Sprinkle some flour on to your work-surface. Cut the dough in half and roll half of it out until it is about 5mm (⅕ inch) thick.

5 (A) Using the large cutter, cut the dough into shapes of your choice. Using the smaller cutter, cut a hole in the centre of each shape. Use a palette knife to lift the shapes of dough on to the baking sheets – you may need to pop out the centres as you lift them.

6 Put a boiled sweet in the middle of each circle.

7 Using oven gloves, put the trays into the oven and bake the biscuits for 6–8 minutes, or until cooked and slightly golden.

8 Using oven gloves, take the trays out of the oven. Leave to cool slightly. Then lift off the biscuits with a palette knife and leave to cool completely on a wire rack. They are quite brittle so be gentle. Serve the biscuits on a white plate so the centres really stand out.

using cutters

Swedish gingerbread biscuits (pepparkakor)

MAKES 10

These cookies are traditionally made at Christmas in Sweden where it is common to make a gingerbread house, too. If you would like to hang your cookies on your Christmas tree, poke a hole in the top of each one before you cook the cookies, and when they are cool, ice them and then thread some ribbon or string through the holes.

YOU WILL NEED:

INGREDIENTS
- small knob of butter, for greasing
- 175g (6oz) plain flour, plus a little extra for rolling out
- 1½ level tsp bicarbonate of soda
- 1 level tsp ground ginger
- ½ level tsp ground cinnamon
- ½ level tsp ground cloves
- 50g (1¾oz) butter
- 1 large egg
- 85g (3oz) light soft brown sugar
- 1½ tbsp golden syrup
- ½ tbsp treacle
- very finely grated rind of ½ orange

to decorate:
- 100g (3½oz) icing sugar
- lemon juice or warm water
- currants

EQUIPMENT
- grater
- 3 baking sheets
- sieve and large bowl
- knife
- jug
- small whisk
- metal spoon
- clingfilm
- rolling pin
- gingerbread man cutters
- palette knife and oven gloves
- wire rack
- small bowl
- spoon

1 Turn the oven to 190°C/375°F/gas mark 5. Rub 3 baking sheets lightly with a small knob of butter.

2 Sieve the flour, bicarbonate of soda, ginger, cinnamon and cloves into a large bowl. Cut the butter into small pieces and add to the bowl. Rub it in with your fingertips until the mixture looks like breadcrumbs.

3 Crack the egg into a jug, add the sugar, syrup, treacle and orange rind. Mix well with a small whisk. Use a metal spoon to stir this mixture into the flour. As it starts to come together, use your hands to knead it into a ball of dough.

4 Sprinkle a little flour on to your work-surface then tip the dough out and knead it for a minute or 2 until it is smooth. Wrap it in clingfilm and leave to rest in the refrigerator for 10 minutes.

5 Sprinkle a little more flour over the work-surface and, using your rolling pin, roll the dough out to about 5mm (⅕ inch) thick. Dip your biscuit cutters into flour then cut out as many shapes as you can. Use a palette knife to carefully lift the biscuits on to the baking sheets. Gather up any spare dough and knead again into a ball. Roll it out and cut out more biscuits and place on the baking sheets.

6 Use oven gloves to put the trays into the oven and cook the biscuits for 6–10 minutes, or until golden brown.

7 Using oven gloves, take the trays out of the oven. Let them cool for a few minutes, then lift them carefully on to a wire rack and leave them to cool completely.

8 Now make the icing: sieve the icing sugar into a bowl. Gradually add a little lemon juice or water and mix until you have a thick smooth paste. You can use just white icing or if you prefer, add a tiny drop of food colouring and mix well. Use the icing to decorate the cookies and pop currants on for 'eyes' and 'buttons'. Leave the icing to set.

fermentation

During fermentation in a drink, the yeast feeds on the sugar in the liquid to produce carbon dioxide gas. This would normally escape into the air, but if the liquid is bottled before fermentation is complete, some of the gas is trapped inside, which makes the drink fizzy.

ginger beer

MAKES 2.5 LITRES (4½ PINTS)

YOU WILL NEED:

INGREDIENTS
- 225g (8oz) golden granulated sugar
- 25g (1oz) cream of tartar
- 25g (1oz) ground ginger
- 2.4 litres (4 pints) boiling water
- 25g (1oz) dried yeast

EQUIPMENT
- 2 large bowls
- long-handled wooden spoon
- sieve
- muslin or clean tea-towel
- large ladle
- jug
- 4 washed and rinsed ginger beer bottles, each should hold about 565ml (1 pint). It is essential to use the correct ginger beer bottles with metal clip lids. These are available from good chemists or wine and beer making shops. Ordinary wine bottles are not strong enough to contain gas and they may explode!

1 Put the sugar, cream of tartar and ginger into a large bowl.

2 Carefully pour in the boiling water – you may need an adult to help you with this. Use a wooden spoon to mix it all together until the sugar is completely dissolved.

3 Leave the bowl until the mixture is at blood temperature – if you dip a finger into the liquid, it should feel as warm as your finger, but not hotter.

4 Add the dried yeast and stir for a couple of minutes until the yeast is completely dissolved.

5 Set a sieve over another large bowl. Line the sieve with a piece of muslin or a clean tea-towel.

6 **A** Using a ladle, fill the sieve with the ginger beer mixture and leave to strain through the material into the bowl. It will trickle through very slowly so be patient and go back to the bowl every half an hour or so to fill up the sieve.

7 When all the liquid has been strained, remove the sieve. Use a clean jug to dip into the bowl and fill up the ginger beer bottles.

8 Fix the lids on firmly. If you have spilt any liquid down the sides of the bottles, rinse it off and dry them. Leave the bottles in a cool dark place for 24 hours.

9 Be careful when you open the bottles, because the beer will be very fizzy and the mixture may spurt out quite quickly.

melting chocolate

Chocolate is melted in a bowl over a saucepan of simmering water. Be very careful when you melt it not to get it too hot – just keep the water simmering gently rather than boiling.

hot chocolate drink

MAKES 4 MUGS

Instead of cocoa powder, you could try sprinkling grated chocolate or a pinch of ground cinnamon over the top. Alternatively, leave the hot chocolate to cool and serve over ice or with ice-cream.

YOU WILL NEED:

INGREDIENTS
- 100g (3½oz) good-quality plain or milk chocolate (or use half of each)
- 565ml (1 pint) full-fat milk
- 75ml (2½fl oz) double cream, whipped to soft peak stage
- 8 marshmallows (optional)
- a little cocoa, for dusting

EQUIPMENT
- 2 saucepans
- large bowl
- oven gloves
- wooden spoon
- whisk
- jug and 4 mugs
- spoon

OTHER THINGS TO DO WITH MELTED CHOCOLATE
- ✔ scoop little balls of ice-cream and stick a small lolly stick into the middle of each ball, then freeze until solid. Dip the balls of ice cream into melted chocolate and then freeze again until set
- ✔ half dip cookies or flapjacks into melted chocolate
- ✔ half dip large nuts, such as Brazil nuts, or pieces of mango into melted chocolate

1 Half fill a saucepan with water and bring up to a gentle simmer. Break the chocolate into small pieces and put into a bowl. Rest the bowl in the pan so that the bowl sits above the simmering water but doesn't touch it.

2 **A** Leave for about 4 minutes until the chocolate has melted. Take the pan off the heat and using oven gloves take the bowl off the saucepan. Give the chocolate a gentle stir with a wooden spoon until it is smooth and glossy.

3 Put the milk into a saucepan and bring just up to boiling point without letting it boil. Remove from the heat. Add a little of the milk to the chocolate, stirring constantly with a whisk until you have a thick paste. Pour over the rest of the milk and whisk until the mixture is slightly frothy.

4 Carefully pour the mixture into a jug, then pour it into the mugs. Spoon the whipped cream on top of the hot chocolate. Put 2 marshmallows on the top of each mug and sprinkle over a little cocoa powder.

caramel

Caramel is sugar that has melted into a liquid that is then cooked to a golden brown colour. It can be used to top puddings, such as crème brûlée, or, once hard, it can be crushed up and added to puddings such as ice-cream. The temperature at which sugar starts to caramelize is very hot – 170°C (325°F) – if you have a sugar thermometer use it in this recipe. If, by accident, any of the caramel splashes on to your hand (or anywhere else), quickly put your hand into cold water.

honeycomb

MAKES AROUND 30 PIECES

This is particularly delicious sprinkled over ice-cream or bash into large chunks that are then half dipped each piece into melted chocolate.

YOU WILL NEED:

INGREDIENTS
- small knob of butter, for greasing
- 4 heaped tsp bicarbonate of soda
- 300g (10½oz) golden granulated sugar
- 6 tbsp golden syrup

EQUIPMENT
- approx 15 x 28cm (6 x 11 inch) deep-sided rectangular roasting tin
- tea-towel
- small bowl
- whisk
- heavy-based deep-sided saucepan
- wooden spoon
- oven gloves
- rolling pin

1 Rub the base and sides of the tin with a little butter. This will make it easier for you to take the honeycomb out of the tin.

2 Put a tea-towel on the work-surface. Put the bicarbonate of soda into a small bowl, next to the tea-towel, and have your whisk ready for when you take the pan off the heat.

3 Put the sugar and golden syrup into a large saucepan and mix together well with a wooden spoon.

4 Put the pan on to the hob over a gentle heat. Stir constantly until the sugar and syrup have completely melted, then turn the heat up a little until the mixture is golden and bubbling – don't let it get any darker or it will taste burned. It will take about 4–6 minutes from the moment you put the pan on the heat to the time you take it off.

5 Using your oven gloves, take the pan off the heat, and put it on the tea-towel. Remove the wooden spoon.

6 Sprinkle the bicarbonate of soda over the mixture and whisk it in quickly but firmly – it will immediately start to bubble up and increase in volume.

7 Holding the pan with your oven gloves, carefully pour the hot mixture into the prepared tin – get an adult to help you with this bit.

8 Leave the honeycomb to set for at least 3 hours, then use a rolling pin to bash it into bits. Store in an airtight container.

Index